THE FATHER WANTS TO HEAL YOU

The Father Wants to Heal You

A Retreat with the Lord's Prayer

NIGEL WOOLLEN

VERITAS

Published 2022 by
Veritas Publications
7–8 Lower Abbey Street
Dublin 1
Ireland
publications@veritas.ie
www.veritas.ie

ISBN 978 1 80097 027 4

10 9 8 7 6 5 4 3 2 1

A catalogue record for this book is available from the British Library.

All Scripture quotations taken from the *CTS New Catholic Bible*, Catholic Truth Society, Publishers to the Holy See, 2007.

All Catechism excerpts from the *Catechism of the Catholic Church*. Copyright © 1994 Veritas–Libreria Editrice Vaticana. All rights reserved. Used with permission.

Cover designed by Jeannie Swan, Veritas Publications
Typeset by Padraig McCormack, Veritas Publications
Printed in the Republic of Ireland by SPRINT-print Ltd, Dublin

Veritas books are printed on paper made from the wood pulp of managed forests. For every tree felled, at least one tree is planted, thereby renewing natural resources.

To the memory of my parents, Rosemary and Anthony, who each in their own way reflected the love of the Father.

'How can you repay them for what
they have done for you?'

Ecclesiasticus 7:28

Contents

Acknowledgements

Grateful thanks to Dr Maria Power for understanding the writer's travails; Fr Chris Hayden (Ferns) for many useful insights; the 'Mad Musicians', Julia and Rachel, for much support and coffee; the 'Jackson Five' of Lackagh (Co. Galway) for faithful friendship; Kelly (Winnipeg) for always keeping me on her 'pray-dar'; Mary-Louise and Enda for help in time of need; and the Veritas family.

Preface
Miracle Prayer

Look to the stars

'Why are you so worthless in your own eyes and yet so precious to God?'

Those words were written by St Peter Chrysologus in the early fifth century;[1] he was renowned for his short but inspired sermons. So many people have an inbuilt tendency to discouragement, leading to low self-esteem and even depression. We can be bound, rendered helpless by negative thought patterns which seem to proceed in a downward spiral. We often need help to discover our true worth. How can we break this cycle of negativity to find how truly precious we are?

A well-known saying sums it up wonderfully: 'Two men looked out from prison bars. One saw the mud, the other saw the stars.'[2] Our outlook, our way of perceiving the outside world, will determine whether we see the mud or the stars! I'm blessed to live near a park with a fair-sized lake which is only a ten-minute walk from my current parish church. When I take my daily stroll, I realise I can too easily be looking down at the path rather than contemplating the beauty of the sun reflected on the lake surface, and the ducks happily waddling to the water's edge. Too often, we can plod along, rather like the two disciples on the road to Emmaus, 'their faces downcast' (Lk 24:17), and we fail to notice the One who is always walking by our side. How can we find the means for a real *conversion* (in the biblical sense), changing our way of looking so that we can hold constantly before our gaze the wonder of this world and of ourselves?

Everybody's looking for something, the saying goes; we could go further and state that everyone is looking for *the ultimate miracle prayer*, the prayer that's always answered. There are no atheists in foxholes, they used to say in wartime; we might add, there are no atheists in times of stress, whether experiencing an earthquake or watching a penalty shoot-out: everyone prays to their god ... If only there was a prayer that was all-powerful, able to transform the world and work miracles. In the Gospel, we find what Jesus says about prayer: 'In your prayers do not babble as the pagans do ... your Father knows what you need before you ask him. So you should pray like this: "Our Father in heaven ..."' (Mt 6:7-9).

Your Father knows what you need before you ask him: this is our starting point. The eternal, infinitely wise and loving God, who is beyond anything we can grasp or imagine, knows what I need even before I do! If we trust that Jesus came to reveal God as Father and enable us to enter into communication with the Eternal One, then we have found our miracle prayer: the Lord's Prayer, which Jesus himself taught his followers. When we pray in the words Jesus gave us, we become, in a sense, what we already are: children of God. The Father sees his Son, Jesus, in us, and wants to give us everything we need in order to find happiness and salvation. All we have to do, then, is to believe we're loved infinitely, to come to God with confidence and to trust we'll receive everything we ask for, if only we ask with faith.

> The Lord's Prayer is the most perfect of prayers ... in it
> we ask, not only for all the things we can rightly desire,
> but also in the sequence that they should be desired. This
> prayer not only teaches us to ask for things, but also in
> what order we should desire them.[3]

But there's a problem: the very word 'father' can have so many connotations, often negative ones, resulting from hurt and anger with regard to parents, father figures and those in authority. This isn't God's fault, but we project onto him our unhappy affective experiences from the past and we hit a brick wall. There's a massive need in our society for healing with regard to parent figures. Another obstacle is that we don't feel worthy to come into God's presence. Indeed, God is infinitely holy (which means all-Other, completely beyond our experience) but the good news is that he has come close to us in his Son, Jesus. Through the incarnation, he has revealed himself; by appearing in our world as a helpless, vulnerable babe in the manger, he shows us we need no longer fear to be in his presence. He is *Emmanuel*, God with us (cf. Mt 1:23).

'I did not come to call the virtuous, but sinners,' says Jesus (Mt 9:13), when the tax-collector Matthew invites him for a meal. If we're confident of our own righteousness, then we don't need a saviour. If, however, we're sinners – weak, broken people who constantly make mistakes and fall so easily – then we can find hope, since Jesus came to save people like us and he has empathy for us in our weakness (cf. Heb 4:15). We can therefore come into the Father's presence with confidence, since our inadequacies aren't a problem for him. We will even find that his all-powerful love is actually at our service, to help us sort out the mess of our lives. As our friend St Peter Chrysologus puts it:

> Our awareness of our status as slaves would make us sink
> into the ground and our earthly condition would dissolve

into dust, if the authority of our Father himself and the Spirit of his Son had not impelled us to this cry ... "Abba, Father!" ... When would a mortal dare call God *Father*, if man's innermost being were not animated by power from on high?[4]

Turn to me for healing

'I saw the Lord': this is how the prophet Isaiah begins his account of his vision of God in the Temple (Is 6:1-13), 'in the year of King Uzziah's death' – around 640 BCE – as if to contrast the existence of earthly rulers, quickly forgotten, with the majesty of the ever-living God. Yet as with several Old Testament accounts of an experience of the deity, the detail is hazy: 'his train filled the sanctuary'. Even a vision in the Temple doesn't seem to allow full access to the invisible God himself; it's as if we can't quite catch a glimpse of what is utterly beyond our comprehension. Yet once Isaiah expresses his willingness to be sent (v. 8) – 'Here I am, send me' – the Lord gives the prophet a mission, one which must be important, since it is quoted four times in the New Testament (vv. 9-10): 'Go and say to this people, "Hear and hear again, but do not understand ... make the heart of this people gross ... so that it will not see with its eyes ... and be converted and healed."' This passage is quoted in slightly different form in John's Gospel: 'He has blinded their eyes, he has hardened their heart, for fear they should see with their eyes and understand with their heart, and turn to me for healing' (Jn 12:40).

It must be stressed that God doesn't deliberately set out to blind people's eyes or harden their hearts; rather, his permissive will allows his children to be free, even to follow paths which will lead them away from him. But the appeal is clear: when we turn back to God, he will heal us! So if we seek the living God, he will lead us on a journey to wholeness, healing and salvation. Remembering that Jesus said in the Gospel, 'To have seen me is to have seen the Father'

(Jn 14:9), we know that following Jesus will lead us to experience the Father's healing touch, for he is the Way to the Father.

'The Son of Man has come to seek out and save what was lost' (Lk 19:10): Jesus pronounces these words after another tax-collector, Zacchaeus, invites him to his home and expresses his desire to change his life. It's good to keep in mind that, in the biblical worldview, the words *heal* and *save* are often used interchangeably: we can affirm the Lord wants to heal us, and has the power to do so, if only we would ask him.

A personal retreat

There are various books on healing parental wounds, written by people more qualified than me on the subject. This book is simply a kind of personal retreat based on the Lord's Prayer from the point of view of healing, since we know it contains all we need to live to the full the kind of life God wants us to live. As we think on this prayer, we will discover that in order to find the Father, we need to encounter his Son, Jesus, who gives us his Holy Spirit, the Spirit who prays within us, 'Abba, Father' (Rm 8:15). With the help of the *Catechism of the Catholic Church*, which ends with a beautiful commentary on the Lord's Prayer (CCC, 2759–865), we consider how saints and scholars through the ages have meditated on this prayer of all prayers. We will also explore how the seven sacraments seem to correspond to the seven clauses of the Our Father (as divided up here), thus strengthening our understanding of the healing power of God's love.

May our efforts in contemplation and study of this miracle prayer help us to meet the gentle touch of our Creator and Father – as did St Ignatius of Antioch, who wrote, not long before his martyrdom in Rome: 'Within me is the living water which says deep inside me: "Come to the Father."'[5] May the Father of goodness himself speak to our hearts, as we seek his face and ask for his guidance on our journey to the kingdom.

———

It may be useful to compare three English versions of the Lord's Prayer (Mt 6:9-13).[6] The first is the one familiar to all Christians, which dates from the sixteenth century; the second is from the Bible translation currently used in the lectionary at Mass; the third is not really a translation as such, but a word-for-word version which is thus closest to the original Greek.

1. **Liturgical tradition (Roman Missal)**
   Our Father, who art in heaven,
   hallowed be thy name;
   thy kingdom come,
   thy will be done
   on earth as it is in heaven.
   Give us this day our daily bread,
   and forgive us our trespasses,
   as we forgive those who trespass against us;
   and lead us not into temptation,
   but deliver us from evil.

2. **CTS Bible (Jerusalem Bible version)**
   Our Father in heaven,
   may your name be held holy,
   your kingdom come,
   your will be done,
   on earth as in heaven.
   Give us today our daily bread.
   And forgive us our debts,
   as we have forgiven those who are in debt to us.
   And do not put us to the test,
   but save us from the evil one.

3. **Word-for-word rendering**[7]

   Father of us the [one] in the heavens:
   Let it be hallowed the name of thee;
   let it come the kingdom of thee;
   let it come about the will of thee,
   as in heaven also on earth;
   The bread of us daily give to us today;
   and forgive us the debts of us,
   as indeed we forgave the debtors of us;
   and not bring us into temptation,
   but rescue us from evil.

1.

We are Family

Our Father, who art in heaven

> The Lord is kind and full of compassion, slow to anger, abounding in love.
>
> PSALMS 144:8

> God loves each of us as if there were only one of us.
>
> SAINT AUGUSTINE

Sleepless in Bangalore

It's hot in south India in January! Bangalore[1] is a large city, not the most densely populated in India but bigger even than London or Paris. Finding it impossible to sleep, my mind turned to the eternal dilemma of how to balance the relationship between God, self and others. Not reaching any meaningful conclusions, I blearily surfaced in the morning for a visit to St Patrick's Church, where our small group was warmly welcomed by the pastor.

After a tour of the magnificent edifice (where I spotted some interesting *ex voto* plaques, including a memorial to a Captain Curley from Ballinasloe in Ireland, benefactor of the church), we

were invited to the parish office for coffee. My gaze was drawn to
a poster on the wall, where these words were written:

> I sought my soul but my soul I could not see.
> I sought my God but my God eluded me.
> I sought my brother and I found all three.
>
> *An unknown prisoner in Siberia*

I felt that my sleepless night had been worth it: somehow the
Lord had given me a glimpse of what I was looking for! That
anonymous prisoner in Siberia, in the midst of unimaginable
hardship, had expressed something that still resonates for us today.
This gives us the sense of why we say *Our* Father: it's not just
about me and my God, but *us*. The very first word of the Lord's
Prayer encourages us to embrace our brother, our sister, indeed the
whole human race.

This reality, an essential starting-point for our journey to
healing, is both a consolation and a challenge. When I pray, I'm
not alone; the very act of pronouncing 'our' reminds me of this.
From the first word of my effort to enter into contact with the
One who has already inspired my prayer through his Spirit, I find
a family. At once I am united with all believers, with countless
friends of God throughout the world – all Christians, and surely,
in a wider sense, all those who seek a relationship with the God
of love – and I find a support, a bedrock and hopefully a path of
healing for my own family as well. As Pope Francis stated at the
2018 World Meeting of Families, 'The Church is the family of
God's children, and God wants every family to be a beacon of the
joy of his love in our world.'[2]

How many times is the Lord's Prayer recited each day? Even
a conservative estimate, starting with the number of Masses
celebrated around the globe (something approaching four
hundred thousand) plus rosary prayers, Liturgy of the Hours,

and so on, would probably run into the millions. Of course, it's not the quantity of prayers recited which matters to God, but the desire of our hearts to respond to his invitation. My *consolation* is in knowing that I can rest, in a certain sense, in the united heart of so many believers and friends of God, since my poor prayer is raised up to the throne of mercy in the company of a worldwide family! Then, if we also count the reality of 'so many witnesses in a great cloud on every side of us' (Heb 12:1), our friends the saints, we can truly be at peace, in the assured knowledge that we are stronger together, and each of us is a 'link in the chain, a bond of connection between persons,' as St John Henry Newman put it so well.[3]

The *challenge* of the 'our' is that we cannot be indifferent to others when we turn to the Lord. Thinking once more of our Siberian prisoner's words of wisdom, we are impelled – through the grace of our common priesthood as baptised Christians – to bring the whole human race before the Father when we pray. This is affirmed in the very first sentence of the Pastoral Constitution of the Second Vatican Council on the Church in the Modern World: 'The joys and the hopes, the griefs and the anxieties of the people of this age, especially those who are poor or in any way afflicted, these are the joys and hopes, the griefs and anxieties of the followers of Christ.'[4] Claiming our dignity as members of God's family helps us to think of others as our brothers and sisters. Above all, the knowledge that God is family encourages us to look upon our own families and the human family in a new light.

Happy families

In recent decades, many theologians and biblical scholars have emphasised (perhaps more than in the past) that God is family. All reflection on the Trinity runs the risk of becoming too abstract and other-worldly to have any real meaning for us, but two simple principles can help us to grasp something of the nature of God:

- the persons are defined by their relations; the Father is Father insofar as he fathers the Son, eternally; the Son is Son insofar as he receives his being eternally from the Father.
- each of the persons in the Trinity is gift for the other; there is infinite, mutual self-giving between the Father and the Son, in the Holy Spirit, who is the very gift.

When we think of our own families, we see parallels: each person in a family is defined by relationship (father, sister, daughter or son, and so on); and we are called to make of our lives a gift for others, for it is by a sincere gift of self that we find ourselves.[5] We remember with affection those people (in our own and in other families) who inspired us because we knew they were 'givers'. Such witnesses, whether explicit believers or otherwise, reflected in some way the love of our heavenly Father. As a young mother put it to me once, 'the greatest gift you can give to your children is your time'. It's a challenge for us when we see non-believers who are more selfless and giving than we are – this takes us beyond our religious categories, remembering the words of the king in a parable told by Jesus: 'In so far as you did this to one of the least of these brothers of mine, you did it to me' (Mt 25:40).

The opposite is sadly true: when we live for ourselves and become takers, we don't reflect God's self-giving love for others, and we don't truly find ourselves. We can all think of certain public figures, celebrities or leaders in society, whose lives are the constant focus of media attention; behind the facade of beautiful people one can often sense a profound *ennui*, the sadness of those who externally have everything yet deep down – we suspect – find themselves empty, deprived of something meaningful to live for. It's likely that such folk didn't have good role models themselves; we can only entrust them to the mercy of God, who knows all the hurts of his children and the mistakes they have made, yet who is always at work to bring about salvation, for he 'wants everyone to be saved and reach full knowledge of the truth' (1 Tm 2:4).

Whatever our family circumstances, each of us is called to become a *gift for others*, and this changes everything, bringing us true freedom! Most of us have read or heard testimonies by others who have found the Lord after some searching, frequently in the wrong places. A common thread would seem to be: someone does bad things, ends up in a desperate plight, through which they feel the need to cry for help to God – who responds by revealing his kindness and mercy, and thus the person finds healing and peace. In some, often unspoken way, this cry echoes that of the prodigal son in the Gospel story, who 'came to his senses' and exclaimed, 'I will leave this place and go to my father' (Lk 15:17-18). This is the trajectory of each of us when we decide to avail of the sacrament of reconciliation: we resolve to *leave this place* of sin and self-centeredness, in order to seek the one we can dare to call Father. We mustn't forget that our 'coming to our senses' is a result of God's grace, often won for us by the prayer of many hidden souls, who bring to their loving Father all those sorely in need of finding a light to guide them home. We tend to seek freedom by doing what we want, yet when we realise that what God wants is much better for us, we start to experience authentic freedom, and a path to healing opens up for us.

Finding peace

At the birth of Jesus, the angels announce to the shepherds: 'Glory to God in the highest heaven, and peace to men who enjoy his favour' (Lk 2:14). This verse should be familiar to us, for it begins the Gloria we sing or recite at Mass each Sunday, in a slightly different translation ('Glory to God in the highest, and on earth peace to people of good will') – but how often do we stop to think what the angels really mean? We should really insert a 'therefore' after the 'and': in other words, we find peace on earth when we seek to give glory to God who is in heaven! The Father wanted his children to live in peace, that's why he sent his own Son to reveal the face of God; Jesus is the Prince of Peace – so when we pray in his name, we are already on the way to living a life of peace and becoming peacemakers for others. Even if we feel too busy to pray or too stressed to stop, the recitation of the Our Father only takes about twenty seconds at normal speed;[6] even saying this prayer once can help us to focus on the presence of our Creator who will never leave us, and yearns for us to be 'people of good will', so that he can shower us with blessings and 'guide our feet into the way of peace' (Lk 1:79). The Catechism states:

> When we pray to the Father, we are in communion with him and with his Son, Jesus Christ (cf. 1 Jn 1:3). Then we know and recognise him with an ever new sense of wonder. The first phrase of the Our Father is a blessing of adoration before it is a supplication. For it is the glory of God that we should recognise him as 'Father,' the true God. We give him thanks for having revealed his name to us, for the gift of believing in it, and for the indwelling of his Presence in us.[7]

Jesus told his disciples – and tells us at the same time – 'As the Father has loved me, so I have loved you' (Jn 15:9); this extraordinary statement is worth pausing over. From all eternity the Father loves his Son, Jesus, infinitely, in a communion of never-ending joy and celebration; to think that each of us is loved in the same way is mind-boggling! Once we grasp this central reality of our existence, we long to know more, to discover how we can experience this love through the light and shadow of each day, till we leave this earth on our last day to encounter love in its fullness.

Let there be chocolate!

In a parish far, far away (in the Indian Ocean) where I was once stationed, I was preaching one Sunday about God's creative word: 'God said, "Let there be light", and there was light' (Gn 1:3). I tried to explain the difference between a word proclaimed by God and by us: if I were to say, for example, 'Let there be chocolate', sadly no chocolate would appear. Someone must have been listening: the next day, when I started Mass, the altar was covered in chocolate bars! Slightly irregular from a liturgical perspective, but the person had made their point with humour. The God who loves bestowing gifts on his children constantly wants to render us able to receive his ultimate gift: the Holy Spirit who prays in us, 'Abba, Father!' (Rm 8:14).[8] If we could only be like small children, calling on *Abba* with total confidence, we would truly begin to live a new life.

'If only you knew what God is offering', says Jesus to the Samaritan woman (Jn 4:10). If only we knew how much the Father wants to give gifts to us and to each of his children – not in the way of a Father Christmas, who randomly distributes presents with a kind of indifference – but with personal, unique blessings tailor-made to fit our needs. We suspect that the Samaritan woman was a deeply wounded person; her private life seems to have been a succession of failures in relationships, she is probably despised and looked down on by many 'right-thinking' members of her community and she possibly clings on to her current partner out of desperation and the fear of being alone. Yet this is the person to whom Jesus chooses to reveal his identity, as well as the Father's gift. So, whatever our hurts from the past or broken relationships, we can approach God with childlike confidence, for he is our Father!

Heaven in your heart

'Heaven'– the goal which is the ultimate gift – must be an important word for Jesus, since it's one of the few keys words that appears twice in the Lord's Prayer. Saint John XXIII recommended we should think every day about the four last things: death, judgment, heaven and hell.[9] For most of us, it's probably easier to imagine hell than heaven; for example, picture sitting in a dentist's chair for all eternity. A dentist I used to go to in Ireland was quite a character, and a serious thinker about religious matters; he seemed to take a mischievous delight in waiting till I was pinned to his chair, rendered mute by a mouthful of pads, before asking deep theological questions. One day he queried, 'What's the difference between salvation and redemption?' 'Er, good question', I replied airily, 'I'll go and research that one.' With the help of enlightened theologically-minded friends, I was eventually able to give an answer of sorts: we could say that redemption (the concept of being 'bought back', paid for) is won for the whole human race by the sacrifice of Christ on the Cross; *everyone* has been redeemed since he paid the price of our deliverance. Salvation is actually rarely defined by the Church; we could say it's a process, through which we are invited to claim our free gift of access to heaven by the power of Jesus' death and resurrection, but we're also free to decline.

So then, if someone were to ask me, 'Are you saved?', I would tend to reply, 'I'm *redeemed*, because of what Jesus did for me on the Cross, but like St Paul, I'm working out my salvation with fear and trembling' (cf. Phil 2:12-13). Paul also states, 'We are not saved yet' (Rm 8:25). Once we understand salvation as a *process* – with past, present and future aspects – we find hope, since past mistakes can be entrusted to God's mercy; we avoid presumption, since we are encouraged to grow in grace; and we are able to look upon our world with new eyes, believing that 'as a father has compassion on his sons, the Lord has pity on those who fear him' (Ps 102:13). Heaven is offered to us as a free gift, and it's the place where God lives. And if you're baptised, then heaven is in your heart. As St Elizabeth of the Trinity wrote: 'Grant my soul peace. Make it your heaven, your beloved dwelling and the place of your rest. May I never abandon you there, but may I be there, whole and entire, completely vigilant in my faith, entirely adoring, and wholly given over to your creative action.[10]

'The heart is the dwelling-place where I am, where I live … [it] is the place of encounter, because as image of God we live in relation: it is the place of covenant.'[11] The word 'covenant' is a key theme of salvation history, expressing the relationship between God and us: our heavenly Father gives himself completely to us in Christ, and invites us to respond by giving him our very selves, whole-heartedly.[12] 'The symbol of the heavens refers us back to the mystery of the covenant we are living when we pray to our Father.'[13]

Why worry?

'Unload all your worries onto him, since he is looking after you' (1 Pt 5:7) – this is good to hear, but not always easy to put into practice! We all know people who aren't really happy unless they have something to worry about. It's good to invite the Father into our 'worry zone', since he wants to bring us out of it to a place of serenity. It may be useful to list our short-term and long-term worries, and to distinguish those we have no control over from those we can do something about. They say we get more anxious as we get older; this may be true. Maybe that's why Jesus asks us to become like little children: when we know that *Abba* is looking after everything, we can learn to trust and let go.

Starting out on our journey towards healing from anxiety, the following practical steps may help: count our blessings, and include all that God spares us from.[14] Think of serene people we know. Call on the intercession of the Blessed Virgin Mary and the saints, who didn't have worry-free lives! Above all, *think of the love* of our heavenly Father revealed by Jesus, who teaches us to call God *Father* and who is in his very self the bridge between heaven and earth, the means of communion with the invisible God. 'Think of the love that the Father has lavished on us, by letting us be called God's children, and that is what we are' (1 Jn 3:1). The goal of this book is to rediscover the Lord's Prayer in a living, dynamic way; if we could only pray this prayer as Jesus wants us to pray it, we would find the healing and peace we crave.

New creation

It's appropriate that the first line of the Lord's Prayer should be associated with the sacrament of baptism, the first of the seven sacraments of the Church and the foundation of the Christian life. Jesus can call God his Father because he is the eternal Son; through the gift of baptism, we are adopted as God's children (cf. Rm 8:14-16; Gal 4:4-7). When Jesus was baptised by John in the river Jordan, 'he saw the heavens torn apart and the Spirit, like a dove, descending on him. And a voice came from heaven, "You are my Son, the beloved; my favour rests on you".' (Mk 1:10-11). This is my favourite Gospel reading used when I officiate at baptisms, as I try to express the gift of God who calls us to be his children. Benedict XVI puts it rather better:

> In Baptism, the heavenly Father also repeats these words for each one of these infants. He says: 'You are my child.' Baptism is adoption and admission into God's family, into communion with the Most Holy Trinity ... These words are not merely a formula; they are reality. They mark the moment when your children are reborn as children of God. From being the children of human parents, they also become the children of God in the Son of the living God.[15]

Of all the sacraments, baptism is possibly the one which involves the least arduous effort from the minister with the greatest effects! A priest I know baptised his own mother, a joyful event which causes us to reflect on the unfolding of God's plan in time: she gave him life, then many years later, he was instrumental in giving her new life in Christ. Through baptism we become a new creation; every time we recite the Lord's Prayer, we are in a certain way renewing our gratitude towards the one who wants us to call him Father, and who says to each of us; My child, 'you are with me always and all I have is yours' (Lk 15:31).

2.

Our Real Identity

Hallowed be thy name

Be proud of his holy name, let the hearts that seek the
Lord rejoice.

PSALMS 104:3

Therefore, you seek, first of all, the glory of God when
you say: *Hallowed be Thy name.*

SAINT THOMAS AQUINAS

Take off your shoes!

In the book of Exodus, Moses 'led his flock to the far side of the
wilderness and came to Horeb, the mountain of God' (3:1). The
passage relates how an angel (which in Scripture often implies the
Lord himself) appeared to Moses in the burning bush which is
blazing but not being burnt up. As Moses goes forward to look,
God calls to him, saying: 'Come no nearer. Take off your shoes, for
the place on which you stand is holy ground' (3:5).

Horeb, the mountain of God – which is possibly another
name for Mount Sinai – is where Moses will receive the Ten
Commandments from the Lord. But firstly, he witnesses this

curious phenomenon of the burning bush, understood (particularly in the tradition of the Eastern Churches) as a revelation of the glory of God, in the form of light – and also points, far into the future, to the virgin birth of Christ from Mary.[1] Moses, awestruck by this proximity to the living God, covers his face. God then gives him a mission to lead his people out of the land of slavery, whereupon Moses, thinking ahead to how he will explain this event to the Israelites, plucks up the courage to make a request: 'If they ask me what his name is, what am I to tell them?' God replies cryptically, 'I Am who I Am' (3:13-14).

Take off your shoes: this action – repeated even today in many churches and other places of worship – shows respect for God's presence, reminding us that we are on holy ground. We could also say that removing our footwear is part of letting go of our own will and desire for control; we are thus rendered more vulnerable and a little poorer. Many pilgrimage sites incorporate a space where pilgrims traditionally walk barefoot (one recalls Fátima, Croagh Patrick in Ireland, the Slipper Chapel in Walsingham[2] and various other shrines) as a penitential gesture, not so much seeking suffering for its own sake as striving to go out of our comfort zone to meet the Lord. Another aspect of this 'discalced' state which may not be immediately obvious: when we take off our shoes, we are relaxing, letting go of formality! I like to think that meeting the *God-with-us* involves feeling at home, since we are with our divine friend, who longs for us to rest in his presence. Throughout the Bible, and indeed in the Christian life of each person, we experience a tension between the awesome otherness of God, who is beyond anything we can grasp, and the nearness of the one who is love, calling us into relationship with him, in order to bring healing to all our human relationships. 'Great in your midst is the Holy One of Israel' (Is 12:6): the paradox for the chosen people, of how the one who is all holy, entirely separate from human experience, can be in the midst of his people, finds its solution ultimately in the incarnation. In Jesus, the very God with us, we find the fullest revelation of the name of the invisible God: Jesus comes to show us that God is our Father, and prays to him on our behalf: *Hallowed be thy Name!* 'May your name be held holy' – in other words, may your name be revered and treated with respect.[3]

So Moses has received some kind of answer, which possibly doesn't satisfy his people: God reveals his name as 'I Am who I Am', which could also be translated from the Hebrew, 'I will be who I will be', then in Greek, 'I Am the One who Is'. Whichever version we select gives us a sense of the infinite, of something we can never contain or possess; all our efforts to pin down God's mystery into something we can define or enclose will inevitably fall short. Yet this doesn't mean we can't grow in an understanding of who he is. Whereas so many of our contemporaries might feel that all one can say about God is that 'there must be something up there', we can affirm in faith that God wants to reveal his beauty and love to those who seek him with a sincere heart. Simply by praying the Lord's Prayer, we grow in our desire to live in a way which brings honour to his name, and to avoid any conduct which would prevent others from wanting to know him too. Jesus himself promised, 'If you believe you will see the glory of God' (Jn 11:40); when we take that step in faith towards him, trusting that we are loved uniquely by the one who can bring us healing, we learn a little more about who we are, and who he is.

The day my uncle met the Beatles

On 26 October 1965, the Beatles were invited to Buckingham Palace, to receive their MBEs from Queen Elizabeth II. That day, there were about two hundred people receiving awards, including my uncle, Mum's brother; as his surname began with a 'B', he was just behind the Beatles in the queue, so he got to meet them. My uncle was quite an amazing man: he'd just brought his young family back to England from West Africa, where he worked as a doctor for several years. He devised the first portable dialysis machine that was in general use (as I only have one kidney myself, this is something close to my heart, you might say).

What most people didn't know at the time my uncle got his MBE was that he was already seriously ill with cancer; he died some fifteen months later aged thirty-nine, leaving his wife with four young children. Now in the time between his award and his death, I was born. You may be thinking: this family history is all very interesting, but what's it got to do with the subject under discussion? Well, my uncle's name was … Nigel – so I was named after him. He only saw me once before he died, but was apparently delighted that his name was to be continued in the family!

Names are important. Each of us has a given (or 'Christian') name – which usually we didn't choose[4] – which implies that each of us has a unique identity whose depths are known only to God. When we take off our shoes (metaphorically speaking) we not only grow in an awareness of the divine in our midst, we also hopefully become more receptive to God's presence in others – since each person is a 'holy land', a sacred space we mustn't trample over unthinkingly, especially with regard to those who are poor or vulnerable.

Epiphanies of beauty

We hear a certain refrain regularly in the Bible, 'Sing a new song to the Lord' (Ps 95:1 and 97:1, for example). Leaving aside the challenge that most parishes have of learning new hymns (striving for a balance between the familiar and the innovative), there is a haunting question which arises now and then in various cultural milieux: *Are there any new songs to be written?* As a (very) amateur composer of hymns, this query intrigues me. Cynics of my generation, comparing contemporary pop songs with the classics of earlier decades, would conclude that all the great songs have already been produced. Mathematicians might comfort us by demonstrating that literally millions of different combinations of notes can be formed by just a few seconds' music. There is a deeper question here, which touches all art forms and concerns the mystery of what it means to be human. God is creator, and made us in his image, which implies that we are a creative lot! Saint John Paul II dedicated his *Letter to Artists* (1999) 'to all who are passionately dedicated to the search for new "epiphanies" of beauty so that through their creative work as artists they may offer these as gifts to the world'. He then quoted the first chapter of the Bible: 'God saw all that he had made, and it was very good' (Gn 1:31).

The uniqueness of each person can be affirmed scientifically – think of fingerprints or iris scans, not to mention face recognition technology – and also anecdotally; I once recognised a casual acquaintance (whose appearance had changed completely) after seventeen years, by his walk! Now we're not all called to write songs or produce sculptures, but we can all make a mark because each of us is a new revelation of God's infinite mystery; every one of us has something new and creative to offer to the world about the one who brought us into existence. We could say that everything about the Father's creative power is *bespoke*; nothing is mechanically churned out, each of his works is uniquely crafted with infinite love. Jesus stated, 'There are many rooms in my Father's house' (Jn 14:2); this encourages us to dare to hope that there is room for many different kinds of personalities in the kingdom (just consider the saints in their dazzling variety). But then Jesus goes on to say, 'No one can come to the Father except through me' (v. 6): only through Jesus can we truly know the Father, since it is through, with and in Jesus that we were created.

The Lord promises in the book of Revelation: 'to those who prove victorious I will give the hidden manna and a white stone – a stone with a new name written on it, known only to the man who receives it' (Rv 2:17). This must mean that when we strive to be faithful, allowing God's love to conquer our negative tendencies, we will be nourished by him (the *hidden manna* – surely a veiled reference to the Eucharist) and our true, individual personality will flourish! We will discover our *new name*, our real identity as God's dear children, and all the wounds we have endured will be transformed into fountains of life and healing for others.

'I want to live forever' is a familiar refrain in modern pop culture: the inbuilt human desire for immortality is realised practically in having children, but also by seeking fame (to have a *name*) – but Christ proposes a different way: 'Anyone who eats this bread will live for ever' (Jn 6:58). A constant theme of Church history is that the most obscure 'nobodies' ignored by everyone sometimes become the greatest saints, whose lives are celebrated joyfully throughout the world – and how much more will the glory of the 'least of these brothers and sisters of mine' (Mt 26:40) shine out in the kingdom of heaven. Sister Clare Crockett (1982–2016) was an Irish nun tragically killed aged thirty-three in an earthquake in Ecuador; her teenage desire to be a famous actress has been surpassed by the interest in her story far beyond her native Derry. I never met her but have encountered various people who knew her well; an Irish bishop told me that there were already enough claims of miracles through her intercession to justify a cause for beatification. Through such contemporary witnesses like Sr Clare, God reminds us that a genuine desire to live the Gospel to the full spreads blessings vastly beyond our limited personal circles!

Today I have become your father

The simple act of making the Sign of the Cross to begin our prayer – which we can often take for granted or perform unthinkingly – is itself an act of faith, a powerful means of protection from evil and an expression of our desire to be immersed in the very life of the Holy Trinity. It finds its origin in the command of the risen Jesus to his disciples: 'Go, therefore, make disciples of all the nations; baptise them *in the name of the Father and of the Son and of the Holy Spirit*' (Mt 28:19; emphasis added). Immediately before this mandate (v. 18), he states: 'All authority in heaven and on earth has been given to me' – suggesting that the invocation of the divine name by his disciples will enable them to claim his infinite authority for their mission.[5]

The name 'Jesus' (*Yeshua* in Hebrew) means: 'the Lord saves'; we could even render it as *I am the one who saves*. Saint Leo the Great tells us, 'If he were not true God, he would not be able to bring us healing; if he were not true man, he would not be able to give us an example.'[6] His name is our refuge and strength.

To access this healing we long for, we can consider how the Catechism links the theme of the divine name to the priesthood of Christ:

> In Jesus the name of the Holy God is revealed and given to us, in the flesh, as Saviour, revealed by what he is, by his word, and by his sacrifice. This is the heart of his priestly prayer: 'Holy Father … for their sake I consecrate myself, that they also may be consecrated in truth.' Because he 'sanctifies' his own name, Jesus reveals to us the name of the Father. At the end of Christ's Passover, the Father gives him the name that is above all names: 'Jesus Christ is Lord, to the glory of God the Father'.[7]

Through his priestly character, Jesus *reveals to us the Father's name*. The Letter to the Hebrews reflects on the role of high priest, fulfilled in Christ: 'Nor did Christ give himself the glory of becoming high priest, but he had it from the one who said to him: *You are my son, today I have become your father*' (Heb 5:5, quoting Ps 109:4).

Through baptism, we are a people of priests; we can intercede for the world and call down God's blessings and healing on those who need them most. We could even say that whenever we pray in the name of Jesus, we are allowing the Father to reveal his name to the whole of creation. The sacrament of holy orders, instituted by Christ to continue his saving work until the end of time, enables men to share in a particular way in his priesthood.[8] The priest, although he 'lives in the limitations of weakness' (Heb 5:2), is appointed to offer the fruit of the earth and the work of human hands to God in sacrifice, in such a way that the Father's name will be glorified and his identity revealed to all who seek the truth and thirst for authentic love. The 'priestly prayer of Christ' in St John's Gospel (chapter 17) referenced in the Catechism is, as we shall see later, a kind of summary of the Lord's Prayer. We can note finally that Jesus prays to the Father: 'I have made your name known to the men you took from the world to give me. They were yours and you gave them to me, and they have kept your word' (v. 6). He prays for his friends, the twelve; but he then prays for those who through their words will believe in him (cf. v. 20), down to us today. It's good to know that Jesus has prayed for us, and continues in heaven to intercede for each of us and for all creation, so that the Father's kindness and compassion might be proclaimed and celebrated for all the world to see.

When Jesus prayed, 'Father, glorify your name!', a 'voice came from heaven, "I have glorified it, and I will glorify it again". People standing by, who heard this, said it was a clap of thunder' (Jn 12:28-9) – I was reminded of this passage during Mass early one Sunday morning, when a bolt of lightning flashed at the exact moment of the consecration (of the bread into the Body of Christ): God can speak to us in different ways, manifesting his awesome power but also encouraging us to soldier on in difficult moments. He has become our father, we bear his name and we can be 'humbly proud' to have such a Father! When we strive to live in a way which glorifies his name, we find our true identity as his beloved children, and become messengers to convey his love and kindness to a world in need.

Beatific vision

The psalm used for the Night Prayer of the Church for Sundays (Ps 90)[9] is a powerful protection prayer dear to many Christians: 'Since he clings to me in love, I will free him; protect him for he knows my name' (v. 14). Then the short reading is a kind of foretaste of heaven: 'They will see God face to face, and his name will be written on their foreheads' (Rv 22:4). I like to imagine that one day, in the fullness of the beatific vision, conversing with friends, we will reminisce: 'Remember we used to recite that passage every Sunday night, and now here we are!' *His name will be written on their foreheads*: we will be sealed with the divine image, finally having become through grace what he wanted us to be from all eternity, holy and immaculate before him in infinite love.

3.

To Serve is to Reign

Thy kingdom come

The Lord is king, let earth rejoice.

PSALMS 96:1

It is better to be a child of God than king of the whole world.

SAINT ALOYSIUS GONZAGA

New world

Jesus came to proclaim the kingdom of God; he assured his followers, 'There is no need to be afraid, little flock, for it has pleased your Father to give you the kingdom' (Lk 12:32). The Catechism states boldly: the kingdom *has already come* in Christ's death and resurrection.[1] Through baptism, we share in the royal dignity of Christ; we truly are a people of kings. Yet when we look around us, it's often hard to see the presence of the kingdom in our midst! We all long for a better world, yearning for the day when every human being will allow the Father to reign in their lives and hearts, and the whole of creation will reflect the glory of the unseen God. So where do we begin? How can we bring about the new world all of us desire?

Scripture comes to help and encourage us, since the power of the Word of God renders present what it proclaims. We can start by giving thanks for the reality of the kingdom already in our midst, 'thanking the Father who has made it possible for you to join the saints … he has taken us out of the power of darkness and created a place for us in the kingdom of the Son that he loves' (Col 1:12-13). This is why Jesus can say, 'the kingdom of God is among you' (Lk 17:21).[2] Whenever we pray 'Thy kingdom come' – alone or with the community of believers – we open up new dimensions in our hearts to allow God to reign. Saint John wrote, 'We are quite confident that if we ask him for anything, and it is in accordance with his will, he will hear us; and, knowing that whatever we may ask he hears us, we know that we have already been granted what we asked of him' (1 Jn 5:14-15) – an extraordinary statement, yet which only mirrors the words of Jesus himself: 'Everything you ask and pray for, believe that you have it already, and it will be yours' (Mk 11:24).[3]

This is very different from some kind of wellbeing seminar on confidence and self-assertiveness (even though such events can be helpful, if based on Gospel values). It's humbling that we can play our part in building up the kingdom, simply by prayer, thanksgiving and praise; we can make the infinite God become a little bigger in the eyes of the world! We can recall here the beautiful prayer of St Elizabeth of the Trinity:

> O Consuming Fire, Spirit of Love, come upon me and create in my soul a kind of incarnation of the Word; that I may be another humanity to him in which he can renew his whole mystery. And you, O Father, bend lovingly over your poor little creature; cover her with your shadow seeing in her only the 'Beloved in whom you are well pleased'.[4]

When Mary pronounces her Magnificat (whose words, like the Lord's Prayer, are mostly found in various places in the Old

Testament), she says, 'My soul proclaims the greatness of the Lord' (Lk 1:46): she *magnifies* God's presence, enabling us to see him more distinctly. Quite literally, the kingdom of God is within Mary at this moment, since she bears the King of kings in her womb. In addition, because Mary defines herself as the servant of the Lord (cf. Lk 1:38), we can grasp why the Church proclaims her as Queen, since, as Vatican II stated, to serve is to reign.[5]

So we mustn't be too easily discouraged if we don't yet see the fullness of the kingdom in this world. If we are pessimistic about the state of society, we can all too quickly concur with the sentiment – taken at face value – of the psalmist: 'Let sinners vanish from the earth and the wicked exist no more' (Ps 103:35). Rather, we can turn this prayer into a plea that 'sinners' (including ourselves) may be transformed by grace into children of God, so that wickedness will indeed exist no more on the earth! We can ask the Lord to give us signs of the kingdom in our daily lives; when we start looking for indicators of his presence, even in the most banal situations, we rarely go away disappointed. Several times a week, travelling between the parishes I serve, I drive along Grace Way (reminding me of the gift of God), turn down Almonds Lane (which recalls the Watchful Tree of Jeremiah 1:11) and go past Providence Grove (evoking the manner in which the Father looks after his children) and so on. 'God speaks to man through the visible creation. The material cosmos is so presented to man's intelligence that he can read there traces of its Creator.'[6]

Footprint

Pope Francis challenges us to leave a mark, a footprint, on history – as he exhorted the young people in Kraków: 'Jesus ... who is life, is asking each of you to leave a mark that brings life to your own history and that of many others.'[7] We should be concerned about our carbon footprint – the trace left behind us by what we consume and the journeys we make – yet, even more vitally, we can strive to *leave a mark that brings life*: by a kind word, a smile, a helping hand to those in need, or by a simple recitation of the Lord's Prayer on good days and bad. Recently I was asked to speak at a memorial service for an acquaintance who had died of cancer; not having known her very well, I felt at a bit of a loss about what to say. The one thing that had always struck me about her was what I said: 'If you'd asked Mary how she saw her vocation, she'd have replied that it was to make other people happy.' We can all agree that if there were more people around with this conviction, the world would indeed be a better place!

One day, Jesus was preaching. 'A man in the crowd said to him, "Master, tell my brother to give me a share of our inheritance." "My friend," he replied, "who appointed me your judge, or the arbitrator of your claims?"' (Lk 12:13-14). Jesus is warning against greed and the desire for possessions, but in addition, he is offering a way to go beyond our material concerns: if we consider his question as it stands, who did appoint Jesus as judge and arbitrator (literally, *mediator*)? The Father! Jesus is indeed the one mediator between God and the human race, who will come to judge the living and the dead.[8] By his response, he seems to be inviting his inquisitor to apply his energies rather towards discovering who this Father is, who calls us to 'inherit the light' (Col 1:12). Now, our friend may have had a genuine grievance; we see in our world how wounds caused by family disputes over land and property can cause untold suffering for decades. Becoming aware that we have an everlasting heritage as children of the great King can help us to put earthly woes into perspective, and bring healing to even the most tangled situations. We are called to live life to the full on this earth, while remembering at the same time that Jesus stated before Pilate, 'Mine is not a kingdom of this world' (Jn 18:36).

The concept of Christ as judge may disturb or even terrify us; we think of the parable of the last judgment (Mt 25:31-46), which begins with the Son of Man – explicitly designated as *the King* (vv.

34 and 40) – who 'will take his seat on his throne of glory. All the nations will be assembled before him and he will separate men one from another as the shepherd separates sheep from goats' (vv. 31-2). Growing in the awareness of our royal dignity as children of the Father, we will surely be impelled to see his presence in others, especially in the poor. Saint Teresa of Calcutta would summarise her mission by stressing the five key words of this passage, holding up five digits of her hand: 'You did it to me' (v. 40). When we pray for the coming of the kingdom, God will take our petition seriously by providing many opportunities to share his goodness with others – often in ways we hadn't planned or even thought of. A wise religious brother I know who runs a pilgrim house of welcome often says, with a twinkle in his eye, 'Jesus always rings the doorbell at the most inconvenient moment!'

We find consolation in the words of Jesus: 'Whoever listens to my words, and believes in the one who sent me, has eternal life; without being brought to judgment he has passed from death to life' (Jn 5:24). This is good news! The more we listen to Jesus – speaking to us in the Bible, in the liturgy, through friends and in the ordinary circumstances of our daily lives – the more we grow in believing in the Father who sent him, and we discover, beyond anything we can feel, that the seeds of eternity are already within us.[9] If we were already saints (and this is our destiny) we wouldn't be afraid of death or judgment, since 'fear is driven out by perfect love' (1 Jn 4:18). There are people who appear utterly fearless – the very rich, hired killers, the self-reliant – and then there are those who learn to place all their fears in the heart of the Father, like a child cuddling up to their dad after waking from a nightmare. Jesus calls us his friends, which means he wants to make known to us everything he has heard from the Father (cf. Jn 15:15). If we strive to listen to him, believing in the Father who sent him and expressing our faith in acts of kindness, we can trust that we will hear one day the words of the King of love: 'Come, you whom my

Father has blessed, take for your heritage the kingdom prepared for you since the foundation of the world' (Mt 25:34).

Removing our block of ice

The variant readings of Greek manuscripts at different places in the Gospels are generally of interest only to specialists. However, sometimes real gems shine through, as in an alternative reading for 'thy kingdom come' in Luke (11:2): 'May your Holy Spirit come upon us and cleanse us'[10] – which at the very least indicates a belief among early Christians in the action of the Holy Spirit who brings about the kingdom; both Tertullian and St Gregory of Nyssa quote this reading. We find an echo of the same theme in St Paul, in his reflection on food laws: 'the kingdom of God does not mean eating or drinking this or that, it means righteousness and peace and joy brought by the Holy Spirit' (Rm 14:17). The Catechism cites this passage, stating:

> In the Lord's Prayer, 'thy kingdom come' refers primarily to the final coming of the reign of God through Christ's return. But, far from distracting the Church from her mission in this present world, this desire commits her to it all the more strongly. The end-time in which we live is the age of the outpouring of the Spirit.[11]

The Russian Orthodox mystic St Seraphim of Sarov (1754– 1833) is chiefly famous for his saying, 'Acquire a peaceful spirit, and around you thousands will be saved'. For him, the kingdom of God is equivalent to the acquisition of the Holy Spirit: this is the centrepiece of the whole Christian life (from his famous *Conversation with Nicholas Motovilov*)[12]. So how can we acquire the Holy Spirit? Picture a gigantic boulder of ice, which is blocking the road ahead of you. Your mission (should you choose to accept it) is to remove the ice, in order to continue your journey.

Basically, you have two options: either you start hacking away at
the ice with your small pickaxe, which, you realise quickly, is going
to take hours or even days of hard work ... or you can *wait for the
sun to come out!* The latter costs you no effort at all; the sun shines,
the ice melts and you can proceed happily on your way. This image
suggests how the Holy Spirit works: human effort can only get
us so far, barely making a dent in the huge block of ice (which
can represent any kind of immovable obstacle that's preventing us
from making progress). When we call on the Spirit, he comes to
shine upon our situation; his power can melt the hardest ice and
enable us to continue on our journey.[13]

The Holy Spirit sometimes seems to be neglected in Christian
circles, which may be due to his intangible, invisible nature.
Similarly, the sacrament of confirmation is probably the least
talked about of the seven sacraments, except when it's time to
'get our teens confirmed'. The Spirit, of course, is at work in
all of the sacraments. If we remember that confirmation is all
about receiving the divine gift with a view to public witness and
proclamation of the kingdom of God, then it seems appropriate to
insert it here. Jesus promised to his friends, on the same evening
that he instituted the Eucharist: 'When the Advocate comes,
whom I shall send to you from the Father, the Spirit of truth who
issues from the Father, he will be my witness. And you too will
be witnesses, because you have been with me from the outset' (Jn
15:26-7).

The word 'witness' is a key theme of John's Gospel: the
Spirit witnesses to the person and mission of Jesus throughout
the world, in every time and place. We are invited to play our
part in building up the kingdom by our witness to the Father's
love and the truth of the Gospel message before others. This
seems daunting, impossible even – just like removing our block
of ice! So by welcoming the Holy Spirit in this sacrament (and
reclaiming his grace and power, in the case of those of us who

can barely remember our own confirmation) we can trust that he will furnish us with the words, gestures and attitudes which can melt the hardest of hearts – but always in his time and after his ways of working. So we see that praying 'Thy kingdom come' and imploring 'May your Holy Spirit come upon us and cleanse us' are indeed different ways of expressing the same desire. When we acquire the Holy Spirit (not by our own efforts but by the pure gift of God who responds to our good will and openness to that gift), we find the healing we need, often imperceptibly but profoundly. Then we can learn gradually to become authentic witnesses, knowing that *we have been with Jesus from the outset*: we were thought of and wanted by the Father before the world was made. Ultimately, the Spirit enables us to make our home and find our place of rest in the *Church*, since 'the Church is the seed and beginning of this kingdom'.[14] We can ask the gentle Spirit of God to heal us of hurts resulting from negative experiences with regard to the Church – which is holy yet made up of sinners – recalling that 'nothing is impossible to God' (Lk 1:37).

When we can't pray

If all this seems too abstract or beyond our reach, if we don't feel the kindness of the Father shining over us or the presence of Jesus, if the struggles of daily life take away our peace, we need not be disheartened, since he promised: 'You will receive power when the Holy Spirit comes on you, and then you will be my witnesses … to the ends of the earth' (Acts 1:8). When we consider how the Lord transformed his disciples – an often clueless bunch – into apostles and saints, this gives us hope even for ourselves: our weakness, low self-esteem, sense of failure or whatever might be dragging us down is like a space, an opening, into which the Spirit can come to make his dwelling. Saint Paul asserts elsewhere: 'We teach what scripture calls: the things that no eye has seen and no ear has heard, things beyond the mind of man, all that God has prepared for those who love him.' Then, crucially, he adds: 'These are the very things that God has revealed to us through the Spirit' (1 Cor 2:9-10). God knows we love him, better than we do ourselves; a mere act of trust in the Spirit who is revealing to us inwardly the promise of heavenly joy can help us traverse this vale of tears. Finally, we can repeat the simple last request of the dying Good Thief next to his crucified King: 'Jesus, remember me when you come into your kingdom.' These few words make up one of the most efficacious prayers in history, if we consider their effect. Jesus replied, 'Indeed, I promise you, today you will be with me in paradise' (Lk 23:42-3).

4.
From Prodigal to Redeemed

Thy will be done on earth as it is in heaven

I rejoiced to do your will as though all riches were mine.

PSALMS 118:14

Walk with your feet on earth, but in your heart be in heaven.

SAINT JOHN BOSCO

A path to healing

It seems a straightforward prayer of desire: to want what God wants. So why is it that sometimes this part of the Lord's Prayer can make us feel uneasy? Maybe we have a latent sense that when we hear the phrase 'the will of God' (said with a loud, stentorian voice), this – whatever it is – is surely going to thwart our freedom, control our existence and basically make us miserable! We might know in theory that God's will is good for us. We can look back and acknowledge the times we chose to rebel, and recall the messes we got into. Yet we can still hesitate over this clause, afraid to commit to God's plan and fearful of what our commitment might entail. It's a positive step to acknowledge our reticence, to understand that we need healing, and to have 'the courage to be afraid', as one author wonderfully put it.[1]

In this chapter, we can ask specifically for healing in the following areas:

- from the consequences of following *my* will, which led me astray. This is deceptively straightforward. It's usually easier for us to identify with the prodigal son than with his envious elder brother (cf. Lk 15:11-32). We can, however, be blind to our own failings. It's a good idea to pray regularly on the lines of Psalm 18: 'Who can detect all his errors? From hidden faults acquit me' (v. 13).

- from what is sometimes called 'spiritual trauma', wounds inflicted by those who claimed to be following God's will yet caused tremendous grief for others in their charge. This is unfortunately quite common in Church history. We can think of monasteries, seminaries, relations between bishops and priests and so on, but also the ordinary life of a parish. To suffer at the hands of one in authority who is convinced that he or she is doing the will of God is particularly painful. There are, thankfully, more studies dedicated to this phenomenon in recent years. Suffice it to recall that the Lord wants to heal everything and can do so.

- from wrong ideas about God and his will. If my image of the Father is that of a controlling taskmaster who's only waiting to punish me for stepping out of line, then I won't be able to claim the joy of discovering his wonderful plans for me and his desire to share my everyday life. It's helpful to recall the classic distinction between God's *positive* will (that which he desires) and his *permissive* will: all that he allows to happen – often as a consequence of human sin or the imperfect condition of creation, in its 'slavery to decadence' (Rm 8:21) – with a view to a greater good.

The path to healing, as ever, begins and ends with Jesus. Since, if Jesus (who was true man, with a human will) can say, 'I have come from heaven, not to do my own will, but to do the will of the one who sent me' (Jn 6:38), then this encourages us to find that there is freedom in letting go of what I want in order to discover the plans of the Father, who always has better ideas than mine. Jesus immediately clarifies what it is the Father wants (v. 39): 'Now the will of him who sent me is that I should lose nothing of all that he has given to me, and that I should raise it up on the last day.'

This is the good news! Now when we hear the phrase 'the will of God' we find serenity, since God's will is for us to be his friends. He yearns for us to be raised to a new kind of life on the last day, and even now we are honoured members of his family: 'Anyone who does the will of my Father in heaven, he is my brother and sister and mother' (Mt 12:50). So, the more we strive to do what God asks of us, the more we become siblings of Jesus and thus children of God. And 'by prayer we can discern "what is the will of God" and obtain the endurance to do it'.[2]

Jesus speaks of the Father's will in various places in the Gospel. It would be enriching to read each of these passages (with the help of a concordance[3]), but just one more quote here can help us: Jesus said, 'My food is to do the will of the one who sent me, and to complete his work' (Jn 4:34). This can be a 'hinge-verse' to lead us to the second part of the Lord's Prayer (on 'our daily bread'). Jesus is the one who enables us to fulfil the Father's will; in addition, he is the Bread of Life who reveals to us what true nourishment is. When we want God's will so much that we hunger for nothing else, we will be saints! In the meantime, we can be at peace, since Jesus has brought us healing through his constant submission to the Father's plans. 'Although he was Son, he learnt to obey through suffering; but having been made perfect, he became for all who obey him the source of eternal salvation' (Heb 5:8-9). By his life, we find meaning; his *yes* empowers us to live joyfully, choosing to 'serve the Lord with gladness' (Ps 99:2) for his will brings us life and peace.

Keep calm and carry on

I enjoy reading all kinds of biographies, especially about the saints, but also those concerning favourite pop stars and sporting heroes of my younger days, and even sometimes the lives of really nasty people. Seemingly I'm not alone in this: there are apparently more than 128,000 biographies of Adolf Hitler in existence (one wonders what new angles remain to be covered, frankly). One of the most memorable biographies I ever read was one about St John Bosco (1815-88); I've rarely found a saint whose fatherly kindness radiated so distinctly. 'Don' Bosco himself wrote a life of one of his pupils, St Dominic Savio, in which he tells a delightful story. One day, the twelve-year-old Dominic was playing football with the other schoolboys. John Bosco asked him, 'What would you do if you only had one hour left to live?' Young Dominic replied, 'I'd carry on playing football!' We would probably have had a different reply. Dominic's response surely doesn't come from an attitude of insouciance or indifference with regard to spiritual realities. Rather, it expresses his conviction that *he's in the right place*: he's where God wants him to be. Dominic, who had already expressed a desire to become a priest, would die just two years later, possibly from pleurisy; at the time of his canonisation in 1954, he was the youngest saint in history not to have died a martyr. His attitude recalls the words of a popular prayer-poem: 'May you trust God that you are exactly where you are meant to be.'[4]

Being where we are meant to be: like many aspects of the spiritual life, this seems simple but often isn't! For most of us, doing God's will means simply getting on with fulfilling our daily duty as best we can, which for a busy parent, shop assistant, factory worker or parish priest, is usually self-evident. There are times in life, however, when we feel that our situation doesn't foster growth and worse, even hinders our relationship with God. We are tempted to cry out with the psalmist: 'Bring my soul out of this prison and then I shall praise your name' (Ps 141:8). If only we were somewhere else, doing something we enjoyed or at the very least set free from whatever 'thorn in the flesh' (cf. 2 Cor 12:7) is weighing us down – dead-end job, stressful environment, broken relationship – then we would at last be able to start living again, and devote ourselves to this 'divine will hunting', as it were!

But then we think of St Paul and his companion Silas stuck in prison in Philippi. Despite having been thrown into the inner prison, their feet fastened with stocks, they 'were praying and singing God's praises, while the other prisoners listened' (Acts 16:25). Paul doesn't wait for everything to be rosy before blessing the Lord, on the contrary he is able to grasp the grace-filled opportunity of every moment to transform it into a living sacrifice of praise to the one from whom he receives his being. The classic expression *carpe diem* ('seize the day') isn't found in the Bible, yet it sums up an aspect of Paul's personality quite well. As God's travelling representative he sees each new challenge as an occasion of witnessing to the Father's mercy; one can only wonder what effect this nocturnal hymn recital had on his fellow prisoners. I once stood in cell 18 of Block 11 in the concentration camp of Oświęcim (then Auchwitz) in Poland where St Maximilian Kolbe spent his final days, like a spark of light shining in a place of unimaginable darkness and hatred; how much his praying presence must have brought comfort and hope to those incarcerated with him.

If we feel too wounded, too broken to be able to praise the Lord in the depths of our current plight, we can take heart by recalling the prayers of the saints, the daily hidden offerings of so many martyrs around the world each day and the intercession of the Church for the world in its painful and bereft state. Once more, the '*our*' – the solidarity dimension – of the Lord's Prayer comes to embrace us; we're not alone, and none of our sorrows is wasted. 'You have kept a record of my tears; are they not written in your book?' (Ps 55:9).

Working in tandem

It's been said (rather cynically) that marriage is like a city under siege: everyone on the outside wants to get in and everyone on the inside wants to get out! I thank God for the many married couples I know who, through all their difficulties, witness to God's loving plans in their family life. Equally I give thanks for the single people I meet who, with their own particular difficulties, (when I meet someone who doesn't have any, I'll write a book to let you in on their secret) also testify to God's goodness and fidelity in their daily lives. Of course, there's a difference between embracing the single state as a choice and enduring it as a reality one hasn't chosen. Inspired by a well-known pop song which implied that if only we got married we'd find perfect happiness,[5] I sometimes feel called to say to such friends, 'Don't wait till you're married to be happy!' This can be applied to all our earthly desires, of course: if only I had that new car/phone/house (insert your wish here), then I'd be content. The saints remind us where true happiness lies. As do those blessed people we've met who radiated joy and kindness to warm our cold hearts, truly being lights on the path of our lives – especially when we knew they didn't have it easy. I think of a Franciscan priest I know, the kind of person who walks into a room and you feel as if the sun has come out and you can hear the birds singing for the first time that day; when I learnt something of his difficulties (not least battling cancer) it increased my reverence for him and challenged me to see my small problems in their true perspective.

When we think about the origin of the word 'conjugal' (pertaining to the married state), it helps us understand how the sacrament of matrimony can be related to this part of the Lord's Prayer in particular: etymologically, conjugal means 'same yoke' (*iugum* in Latin), deriving from an Indo-European root whose verb means 'join' or 'unite'. The concept of a wooden beam put between a pair of oxen (or other animals), enabling them to pull together on a load, may seem somewhat archaic for us modern, urban types. We recall, however, the words of Jesus, and we find the connection: 'Shoulder my yoke and learn from me, for I am gentle and humble of heart, and you will find rest for your souls. Yes, my yoke is easy and my burden light' (Mt 11:29-30).

All of us, whatever our state in life, are invited to *shoulder the yoke of Jesus*. As we open up to the Father's will, we learn to become his co-workers for the kingdom. We begin to discover that he does all the hard work, shouldering our burdens and lightening our load. It may be simplistic to suggest that the basis for a happy marriage is when both husband and wife strive to follow God's will – but it's a start. A contemporary equivalent of the yoke might well be the tandem bicycle: the two riders must pedal at the same pace (and preferably in the same direction) in order to go anywhere, but it is permitted for a stronger rider to set the pace, the other one taking things easy. With Jesus, we need to learn to let go! He is the stronger one (cf. Lk 11:22), who knows where he is leading us; our main task is to let go and enjoy the view. 'The Lord will do the fighting for you; you have only to keep still' (Ex 14:14). We ask Mary's prayers for married couples; she who once expressed her joyful desire to do the will of God – 'Let what you have said be done to me' (Lk 1:38) – and later gave her only piece of advice recorded in the Gospels, incidentally at a wedding: 'Do whatever he [Jesus] tells you' (Jn 2:5). Saint Augustine confirms the theme of marriage linked to this clause of the *Pater* in a profound if challenging passage:

It would not be inconsistent with the truth to understand the words, 'Thy will be done on earth as it is in heaven,' to mean: 'in the Church as in our Lord Jesus Christ himself'; or 'in the Bride who has been betrothed, just as in the Bridegroom who has accomplished the will of the Father'.[6]

Finally, we can cite St Charles de Foucauld (1858–1916), whose life story is a most entertaining journey from prodigal son to redeemed child of the heavenly Father. In later life he wrote, 'As soon as I believed there was a God, I understood I could do nothing else but live for him, my religious vocation dates from the same moment as my faith: God is so great. There is such a difference between God and everything that is not.'[7] He also left us this beautiful Prayer of Abandonment:

Father, I abandon myself into your hands; do with me what you will. Whatever you may do, I thank you. I am ready for all, I accept all. Let only your will be done in me, and in all your creatures. I wish no more than this, O Lord. Into your hands I commend my soul; I offer it to you with all the love of my heart, for I love you, Lord, and so need to give myself, to surrender myself into your hands, without reserve, and with boundless confidence, for you are my Father.[8]

Coda: On earth as in heaven

The revised Mass translation in English which appeared in 2011 has raised much comment, yet as far as I'm aware, no one seems to have noticed a significant alteration to the Lord's Prayer (at least in the version recited in Britain, Ireland and several other English-speaking countries): the comma was removed! Instead of pausing after 'earth' – 'thy will be done on earth, as it is in heaven' – we are now invited to pause after 'done' – 'thy will be done' [*pause*] 'on earth as it is in heaven' – as has long been the practice in North America (and, interestingly, in my current parish). The original Greek text of the New Testament contains no commas; every translator has to make an editorial decision based on context and the likeliest meaning. A look at the Our Father in other languages is quite conclusive: in nearly every one surveyed,[9] the pause clearly follows 'thy will be done' – the Americans got it right first time!

Why is this important? Simply, because it highlights a crucial aspect of our prayer: 'on earth as in heaven' applies to the *three preceding clauses*. In other words, what we are really saying to the Father is:

- may your name be revered, on earth as (it is) in heaven!
- may your kingdom come, on earth as (it has) in heaven!
- may your will be done, on earth as (it is) in heaven!

This small but significant change opens up vast horizons. Now that it's clearer for us that in paradise, God's name is revered, his reign acknowledged and his will followed in perfect love, our pining for heaven surely increases and at the same time, our desire that all on earth might live in recognition and acceptance of the Father's loving presence is intensified! 'All the ends of the earth have seen the salvation of our God' (Ps 97:3). While this world is not yet as we'd like it to be (to put it mildly), it is consoling to know that God wants the earth and all of creation to reach the fullness he planned for it from the beginning (cf. Rm 8:19-22). He yearns for us to simply say yes to his loving plans. Wherever there are believers who welcome his gentle invitation to 'shoulder the yoke' of Jesus and allow him to show us the right way to live, our world will slowly be transformed into what the Father wanted it to be from before time began. *And this will happen!* In ways we cannot begin to imagine, the power of the Holy Spirit working in human history, always with complete respect for our free will, moves toward the day when all things will at last be in harmony with his project of salvation: 'his own designs shall stand for ever, the plans of his heart from age to age' (Ps 32:11).

To sum up, we know things will be better (for us and for the whole human race) the more we try to do what God wants us to do. We are weak, it's true; that's why we need to welcome the Spirit of Jesus, who helps us to say yes to God's will and to see more clearly what he is asking of us. Saint Paul sums it up so well:

> The Spirit too comes to help us in our weakness. For when we cannot choose words in order to pray properly, the Spirit himself expresses our plea in a way that could never be put into words, and God who knows everything in our hearts knows perfectly well what he means, and that the pleas of the saints expressed by the Spirit are according to the mind of God. (Rm 8: 26-7)

5.

You are What You Eat

Give us this day our daily bread

They gazed on God. They ate and they drank.

Exodus 24:11

When I want something very much I thank God beforehand, for I feel God will certainly grant what he has been thanked for.

Saint Mary MacKillop

Remedy for all our ills

Now we've reached the second part of the Lord's Prayer: having celebrated the goodness of God and offered him our praise through his Son, we now seem to have 'shifted gears' in a certain sense; this is the section where we are encouraged to tell God what we want! As mentioned in the preface, we should keep in mind the words spoken by Jesus immediately before he teaches this prayer to his disciples: 'Your Father knows what you need before you ask him' (Mt 6:8). The Catechism states: 'Jesus teaches us this petition, because it glorifies our Father by acknowledging how good he is, beyond all goodness'.[1]

It's been said that God has three kinds of responses to prayers of demand:
1. *Yes*: you can have what you want
2. *Not yet*: you'll get it but wait a while
3. *I've got a better idea*: there's a bigger plan.

Imagine if all our prayers were answered immediately: this probably wouldn't be good for us. In fact, an anonymous author wrote in the second century: 'None of the righteous receive the fruits of their goodness instantly, but all have to wait for them. If it were otherwise, if God gave quick rewards for righteousness, then it would not be piety that drove us to good acts but a simple matter of business.'[2] Every parent understands this attitude, constantly having to resist the temptation to give their children everything they demand instantly, which – even if the parent had the means to do so – would surely render their offspring lazy and self-indulgent.

So why should we ask for *bread*? It symbolises the basic need for sustenance – in Mediterranean culture, certainly – but more profoundly, this petition helps us distinguish between what we *want* and what we *need* – and there's a world of difference! I met Cardinal Francis-Xavier Nguyên Van Thuân (1928–2002) in Rome in the mid 1990s. He had previously spent thirteen years in a Communist prison in his native Vietnam, where he would scribble a daily meditation on the only paper available, the back of a tiny 'page a day' calendar in his cell. He would write: 'I will never be able to express my great joy! Every day, with three drops of wine and a drop of water in the palm of my hand, I would celebrate Mass. This was my altar, and this was my cathedral! It was true medicine for soul and body.'[3] (It's related that he spoke with Romanian Cardinal Alexandru Todea, at the 1991 Synod for Europe, about the relative difficulties of acquiring bread to celebrate Mass in prison, in Romania and Vietnam; it must have been moving to overhear such a conversation between two great figures of the persecuted Church.)

True medicine for soul and body: here we find in a simple petition the route to the deepest healing possible. By praying for 'us' (not just 'me') we call to mind those who don't have enough to eat and are urged to do our utmost to help them.[4] We learn something of trusting in providence, as we are instructed to pray for what we need *just for today*. Furthermore, we can glean in an ancient translation of *daily* as 'super-substantial' that Jesus is referring to himself as our Bread of Life, which the Father gives to those who ask him. Really, we're pleading to the Father: *Give us Jesus!* For he is the answer to all our questions, the remedy for all our ills. 'Through his wounds you have been healed' (1 Pt 2:24).

Imagine no possessions

When the chosen people were wandering in the desert, God provided bread from heaven for them to eat:

> The Lord said to Moses, 'Now I will rain down bread for you from the heavens. Each day the people are to go out and gather the day's portion; I propose to test them in this way to see whether they will follow my law or not. On the sixth day, when they prepare what they have brought in, this will be twice as much as the daily gathering.' (Ex 16:4-5)

So they were instructed to collect just enough for each person every day (with two days' worth of portions permitted before the Sabbath), no hoarding allowed! There's a principle we should reflect on every time we pray for what we need today; when we resist the temptation to be hoarders – making sure we always have plenty of supplies in reserve – we give glory to our heavenly Father, since we are making an act of trust in his providence, believing that he is looking after us. Jesus insists:

> I am telling you not to worry about your life and what you are to eat, nor about your body and how you are to clothe it ... your heavenly Father knows you need them all. Set your hearts on his kingdom first, and on his righteousness, and all these other things will be given you as well. (Mt 6:25, 32)

He then adds,

> So do not worry about tomorrow, tomorrow will take care of itself. (v. 34)[5]

Of course, there is a distinction between hoarding and good planning! Parents need to make sure they have enough to feed their children and so on. But as a priest friend is fond of saying, 'Be attitude!' It's all about our *attitude* towards food supplies or whatever we might tend to cling to, learning to let go in order to trust in the Father who knows what we need. Certainly, there are times when our trust seems to be tested to its limits; these moments of challenge help us to go further in learning to depend and can even make us face our need for self-sufficiency. Pope Francis recently proposed St Joseph as a model of faith, saying that he 'teaches us that amid the tempests of life, we must never be afraid to let the Lord steer our course. At times, we want to be in complete control, yet God always sees the bigger picture.'[6]

A priest with whom I used to take meals regularly had known real hunger during his years as a missionary in Africa. One day, when there really was nothing to eat, he went into his small chapel and literally banged on the door of the tabernacle, saying forcefully: 'Lord, I'm hungry!' Immediately, he heard a car horn; some Italian nuns passing by were delivering ample food supplies, enough for him and his parishioners. When you had lunch with this priest, you made sure you finished everything on your plate!

The Lord often uses circumstances to educate us in the ways of trust, as I recall from an episode in Paris some years ago when I'd left my suitcase on the train. As the RER (suburban train) slowly moved away from the platform, I knew it was already too late. Several days of phone calls and online research ensued, not to mention heartfelt prayer (I'm great at intense supplication when I really need something from God). Finally I made my way to an imposing high-security building in a run-down *quartier* of Paris I'd never visited before. After identifying the contents of my trusty old case and reluctantly parting with ten euro, I was handed a large black bin liner, which, as it turned out, contained all my travelling kit. The suitcase itself, however, had been blown up by the French police. In addition, some over-zealous officer – presumably searching for drugs or the like – had very deliberately slashed my Bible cover, sponge bag and the heel of one shoe with a sturdy knife. Otherwise, everything was much as it had been a week previously. It only remained to find a store: a small *maroquinerie* was conveniently located just down the road (surely they were in cahoots with the Force, I speculated). To the bemusement of the shop assistant, I told my sad tale and bought a new suitcase. As I left with my purchase, I could hear her on the phone to a friend telling this tall story of the *anglais* whose case had exploded in custody.

At the time, this episode seemed like a disaster, but looking back, there was nothing in that bag that I still have ten years later (except the Bible). The recalling of this incident encourages me not to react impatiently when other people forget things and also reminds me that so much of what we cling to is transient, temporary. Such experiences help us to move from 'stress to rest', and help us understand a little of what St Paul means when he writes:

Yes, the troubles which are soon over, though they weigh little, train us for the carrying of a weight of eternal glory which is out of all proportion to them. And so we have no eyes for things that are visible, but only for things that are invisible; for visible things last only for a time, and the invisible things are eternal. (2 Cor 4:17-18)

Attitude of gratitude

Jesus knows that most of us find it hard to have eyes for things that are invisible. This is why he often teaches us starting from visible realities, which can lead us to the unseen dimensions of our existence that they point to; this is highlighted in St John's Gospel in a powerful way. The Saviour born in Bethlehem (a name which means 'house of bread') wants to feed his hungry followers, since he is the perfect image of the compassionate Father; how much more he wants us to be nourished by his own divine life, since he is the Bread of Life (cf. Jn 6:34-48).

As alluded to in the previous chapter, when the disciples find Jesus talking to a Samaritan woman, their first thought is to urge him to have something to eat. The Master's reply is disconcerting: 'My food is to do the will of the one who sent me and to complete his work' (Jn 4:34). If we trust that reciting the Lord's Prayer with open hearts changes us to become more like Christ, then we will discover that a sincere desire to do God's will – despite our limitations and weaknesses – can nourish us, and even awaken in us what our souls hunger for above all: the Bread of Life in the Eucharist, which is Jesus himself. Shortly after this episode in John, we find him feeding a large crowd with five barley loaves and two fish offered by a small boy (6:1-15)[7]. Jesus takes the little we offer him, in order to multiply it and nourish a multitude – and there's plenty left over! Note that he 'took the loaves, gave thanks, and gave them out to all who were sitting ready' (v. 11): this reminds us to 'say grace' before meals, giving thanks to the Father for the food we have, and encourages us to make of our lives a thanksgiving sacrifice to the God who wants us to have all we need. 'Eucharist', of course, means 'thanksgiving': I often find that the people who inspire me the most are those who seem to glow with a constant 'attitude of gratitude' towards their Creator, not complaining about all that's lacking but giving thanks for what they have, and simply for the joy of being alive. A cartoon recently depicted St Peter working in his heavenly office, with two large trays on his desk: one was piled high with petitions, while the tray marked 'Thanksgiving' was almost empty. Surely a resolute determination to praise and thank God in all circumstances would provide us with abundant healing, if only we could fix our minds on what we've received instead of bemoaning what we don't have. Saint Paul puts it simply: 'Be happy at all times; pray constantly; and for all things give thanks to God, because this is what God expects you to do in Christ Jesus' (1 Th 5:16-18). We could interpret this as saying: the secret of happiness is to pray constantly and give thanks to God in all things.[8]

But Jesus doesn't limit himself to providing an afternoon meal for this large crowd; he wants them to discover the true Bread that only he can give:

> You are not looking for me because you have seen the signs but because you had all the bread you wanted to eat. Do not work for food that cannot last, but work for food that endures to eternal life, the kind of food the Son of Man is offering you, for on him the Father, God himself, has set his seal. (Jn 6:26-27)

It's true that the Church doesn't describe the sacrament of the Eucharist as a 'sacrament of healing' as it does for reconciliation and anointing, yet various prayers of the Mass underline its healing powers. Just before receiving holy communion, we adapt the words of the centurion in the Gospel (cf. Mt 8:8): 'Lord, I am not worthy that you should enter under my roof, but only say the word and my soul shall be healed.' Then after receiving, the priest privately recites a beautiful ancient prayer: 'What has passed our lips as food, O Lord, may we possess in purity of heart, that what has been given to us in time may be our healing for eternity.'[9] When we discover Jesus as our Bread of Life, we are on the journey to the greatest healing possible this side of heaven!

Mind what you say to children

There was once a young boy called Joe, who wanted to be a priest. He asked his pastor if he could make his first holy communion, but was told he was too young (in those days children received the Lord for the first time at around the age of twelve). The pastor, however, recognising his evident piety and serious nature, suggested he ask the bishop who was about to visit the parish. So Joe made his request to the bishop, who gave the same answer; then, seeing the boy's disappointment he added, 'But when you're the Pope, you can change the rules!'

Well, our friend Joe (full name Giuseppe Sarto) became a priest, then a bishop … and in 1903 was elected Pope, taking the name of Pius X. He didn't 'change the rules' immediately, but seemed to be waiting for a sign from the Lord. One day, he received an English lady for a private audience, accompanied by her four-year-old son, John. When she mentioned her boy's desire to make his first communion, the Pope asked him, 'Whom do you receive in holy communion?' John replied, 'Jesus Christ'. 'And who is Jesus Christ?' 'Jesus Christ is God!' he replied promptly. Pope Pius turned to the mother, saying: 'Bring him to me tomorrow; I will give him holy communion myself.'

I love this story since it demonstrates how the Holy Spirit can work, both through the Supreme Pastor of the Church (now *Saint* Pius X) and also through the hearts of small children! May the joy experienced at every parish first holy communion ceremony stay with us, especially in difficult times, so that we may rekindle our childhood innocence and renew our gratitude to the Father who wants the best food for the children he loves. 'Whoever comes to me I shall not turn away,' Jesus promised (Jn 6:37); may our simple recitation of the prayer he taught us contribute to working for the food that endures to eternal life, and may all God's children have enough to eat and, above all, find access to the Bread of heaven which heals and prepares for the life of the kingdom. 'O sacred feast, in which we partake of Christ: his sufferings are remembered, our minds are filled with his grace and we receive a pledge of the glory that is to be ours.'[10] The example of Blessed Carlo Acutis (1991–2006) – who created a website of eucharistic miracles around the world which is still active today – will surely inspire many young people to discover the healing power of Jesus, the Bread of Life.[11] In our quest for healing and wholeness, we can also call upon the help of the Mother of the Eucharist, whose total availability to the divine plan – body and soul – permitted the Word to become flesh and to remain with his people till the end of time.[12]

Finally, the episode of the disciples on the road to Emmaus reminds us that at every Mass, we receive the glorified, risen Body of our Lord: we are the Easter people! One small detail shows the divine Healer at work: when Jesus handed the bread to them, 'their eyes were opened' (Lk 24:31). Could this point to the healing we need from the consequences of the Fall?[13] When our first parents took the forbidden fruit, their eyes were opened – to realise they were naked (cf. Gn 3:7); now, through the gift of the Risen One, the eyes of his friends are opened to the reality of his victory over death and the promise of new life in him. May our sharing in the Eucharist open our eyes to the beauty of God and his fidelity to the beloved children of his that we are. May we never forget the promise of Christ: 'Anyone who eats this bread will live for ever' (Jn 6:58).

6.

Your Sins are Forgiven

And forgive us our trespasses,
as we forgive those who trespass against us

> O Lord our God, forgive us our sins; rescue us for the
> sake of your name.
>
> PSALMS 78:9

> We all need to be forgiven by others, so we must all
> be ready to forgive. Asking and granting forgiveness is
> something profoundly worthy of every one of us.
>
> SAINT JOHN PAUL II

Light in a dark place

The book of Job in the Old Testament is not exactly easy reading. It's certainly a literary masterpiece, a high point of Hebrew prose, and explores the meaning of suffering – through the trials of the just person, represented by Job – yet its conclusions can leave us feeling bewildered, as if the only explanation for all his hardship is that *God is all*. Bible scholars and preachers tend to sum up this book by clarifying that only in Christ can we find a definitive answer to human suffering, which is certainly true; yet, we come to the end of Job with a nagging sense of dissatisfaction. However, everyone likes a story with a happy ending; the last chapter (42) sees the restoration of Job's material blessings (he apparently fathers ten more children and does rather well materially, acquiring fourteen thousand sheep and so on). An extraordinary claim is made by the sacred author (v. 10), which we can almost miss if we read too hastily: 'The Lord restored Job's fortunes, because he had prayed for his friends.'

This is a profound statement! Job, understood in the full light of Christian revelation, is a biblical *type* or prefiguration of Jesus: as the just man who suffers unfairly, he not only bears his trials patiently, but intercedes for his 'friends' – who don't exactly cover themselves with glory by their attitudes – and thus he enjoys previously unimagined blessings. This verse reminds us of the power of *intercessory prayer*; when we pray for others, there is benefit for us. Even more, if we strive to pray – sometimes with gritted teeth, or even tears – for those who have injured us, we are surely united to Christ, who prayed and found excuses even for those who were torturing him unto death: 'Father, forgive them; they do not know what they are doing' (Lk 23:34). He refers to the ignorance of those who are unwittingly putting to death the Messiah – echoed by St Paul, who proclaims the hidden wisdom of God, 'a wisdom that none of the masters of this age have ever known, or they would not have crucified the Lord of Glory' (1 Cor 2:8). Jesus is praying not just for his executors (who are 'only obeying orders') but for the authorities who gave those orders, for his beloved chosen people and indeed for the whole human race. When we sin, *we don't know what we are doing* in a certain sense; we are oblivious to the hurtful consequences of our unkind words and actions which wound others and even the heart of the Saviour.

While it's true (and a troubling thought for our own particular final judgment) that sin has ripple effects greater than what is visible, fortunately the opposite is even more true! Our efforts to pray and seek the good contribute to the invisible growth of the kingdom, the 'hidden wisdom' of which Paul writes. This takes us back once more to the 'our' in the Lord's Prayer, this solidarity with all believers and in a wider sense with the whole human race, aligning our desire with that of God, who 'is being patient with you all, wanting nobody to be lost and everybody to be brought to change his ways' (2 Pt 3:9). Returning to this key final chapter of Job, we read a few verses later: 'The Lord blessed Job's new fortune even more than his first one' (42:12). I came across this verse in a quite imaginative translation some years ago[1] – at a time of considerable personal tenebrosity – which ran something like this: 'The Lord blessed Job even more in the second half of his life than in the first half of his life.' God's Word truly is a lamp for our steps and a light for our path (cf. Ps 118:105); in times of darkness, our loving Father can shine his kindly light upon us through Scripture – even parts of it which we might think obscure or irrelevant to our situation – to bring us to a better place. As St Peter observed, 'You will be right to depend on prophecy and take it as a lamp for lighting a way through the dark until the dawn comes' (2 Pt 1:19). When we seek to grasp the prophetic nature of the Bible, we may not find the reply to all our queries, but we certainly receive the light we need to keep going, and keep hoping.

Simply to be able to pray, 'Father, forgive us our trespasses' is a profound act of faith, which liberates us, bringing healing and joy – and is part of our prayer for our friends and for the entire world. But I need to believe he can forgive *me* and *you*, not just the human race in some abstract sense. The extraordinary claim of the psalmist – 'He does not treat us according to our sins, nor repay us according to our faults' (Ps 102:10) – appears to contradict every sane principle of distributive justice in salvation history, yet can be understood in the light of divine mercy, which has no limits. We can unite ourselves to the sentiments of the prophet: 'Once more have pity on us, tread down our faults, to the bottom of the sea throw all our sins' (Mic 7:19) – trusting that having done this, the Father as it were puts up a sign, 'No fishing!' When we have been washed of our stains by the Blood of Christ – through the waters of baptism and the sacrament of reconciliation – we give honour to God by not going back to dwell on past mistakes, but rather striving to live in the joyful state of those for whom the slate has been wiped clean, the debt is cancelled and we have been set free.

Meanwhile, back at the house

In a well-known Gospel episode (Mk 2:1-12), Jesus is back home and the whole town seems to be there. Four men carrying a sick friend on a stretcher want to bring him to Jesus but the crowd make it impossible. So they go up on to the roof and make an opening to lower the stretcher (with the poor fellow on it, he doesn't really have a choice) before the Lord.[2] It must have caused quite a stir, this house (possibly Simon Peter's) filled to overflowing with disciples eagerly hanging on to every word of the Master, then the roof caves in! And Jesus, 'seeing their faith' says to the bed-ridden man, 'My child, your sins are forgiven' (v. 5). The scribes are appalled, claiming blasphemy. It would also have been interesting to see the reaction of the sick man's friends; this wasn't quite what they came looking for! But Jesus sees the true need, and also works a physical healing, thus ratifying his authority to forgive sins: 'Get up, pick up your stretcher and go off home' (v. 11).

This short Gospel passage highlights Jesus' ability to heal and forgive, and also reminds us of the power of intercession, as we saw in the final chapter of Job above. Seeing their faith, the Lord works a miracle; we know nothing else about the 'Four Amigos', but their action can inspire us to bring our loved ones – and indeed the whole of suffering humanity – to the feet of Jesus, even if we have to *raise the roof* (implying persistence, creativity and thinking outside the box). We could see these friends as unnamed heroes of the Gospel, a bit like carers in society today. When we pray, we can become 'spiritual carers', leading others to Jesus by our intercession, trusting that he can bring healing and reconciliation, even from a distance.

We see throughout the Gospel, and particularly in the first few chapters of Mark, a kind of *chiaroscuro* – a contrast between light and dark – effected by the Lord's presence. The condition for religious practice among the people of Israel was to be in a state of ritual purity in order to attend worship.[3] So a leper, for example (or someone who touches one), is excluded from the community. Jesus, however, constantly turns everything upside down: he touches the leper, raises the dead girl, allows the woman with a haemorrhage to touch his cloak, and so on. The challenge for the religious leaders of his time is that instead of rendering himself ritually impure (which is absurd, since he is the Author of the Law), Jesus brings healing and purity to those with whom he enters into contact, and even has the power to raise the dead!

We priests regularly meet people who find it hard to believe that God has forgiven them. We encourage them to pray for the grace to forgive themselves, trusting that the Lord has 'cancelled every record of the debt that we have to pay; he has done away with it by nailing it to the cross' (Col 2:14). Some people spend years tormenting themselves by the thought of their past misdeeds; we could look on this as a kind of purgatory, yet the Lord wants us to live in the joy of being forgiven. People who have come back from far away can radiate God's mercy in a powerful way. Didn't Jesus say in the Gospel, 'Every one of men's sins and blasphemies will be forgiven them' (Mt 12:31)? We tend to move too quickly on to the following part of the verse without pausing to consider this extraordinary statement.[4]

Another thought-provoking (and possibly neglected) verse in the New Testament can help us: 'Think of what Christ suffered in this life, and then arm yourselves with the same resolution that he had: anyone who in this life has bodily suffering has broken with sin' (1 Pt 4:1). This can bring some measure of consolation to those who don't obtain the healing they pray for. In addition, it proposes one of several biblical ways of cancelling out sin which appear to fall outside normal sacramental categories. The following verses are particularly relevant to this theme:

> Love covers over all offences. (Prov 10:12)

> Kindness to a father shall not be forgotten but will serve as reparation for your sins. (Eccles 3:14)

> Anyone who can bring back a sinner from the wrong way that he has taken will be saving a soul from death and covering up a great number of sins. (Jas 5:20)

A Gospel passage we can never hear or read too often is the parable of the prodigal son, particularly the father's reaction to his wayward offspring's return: 'While he was still a long way off, his father saw him and was moved with pity. He ran to the boy, clasped him in his arms and kissed him tenderly' (Lk 15: 20). This story told by Jesus expresses something of the joy of our heavenly Father when we decide to come home.

Terms and conditions apply

In chapter 3 we read that Jesus promised, 'Everything you ask and pray for, believe that you have it already, and it will be yours'. However, the following verse provides a foreboding context: 'And when you stand in prayer, forgive whatever you have against anybody, so that your Father in heaven may forgive your failings too' (Mk 11:24-5). His statement finds an echo in this section of the Lord's Prayer, surely its most challenging line:

> This petition is astonishing. If it consisted only of the first phrase, 'and forgive us our trespasses,' it might have been included, implicitly, in the first three petitions of the Lord's Prayer, since Christ's sacrifice is 'that sins may be forgiven'. But, according to the second phrase, our petition will not be heard unless we have first met a strict requirement. Our petition looks to the future, but our response must come first, for the two parts are joined by the single word 'as'.[5]

The small word 'as' is one of the most important in the Bible.[6] We think of the parable of the merciless servant (Mt 18:23-35) whose master, out of pity, cancels his debt of ten thousand talents (think a billion dollars, say) – which reminds us that we could never pay back for our sins by our efforts, nor earn heaven by our merits. Yet this very man shortly afterwards tries to throttle the fellow servant who owed him a hundred days' wages (not a trivial sum, we note, yet dwarfed by the cancelled debt). The result: 'in his anger the master handed him over to the torturers till he should pay all his debt' (v. 34).[7] When we refuse to forgive, we are, in a certain way, torturing ourselves; when we let go of grievances, we become free and can claim God's forgiveness. Of course, this is easier said than done! As C.S. Lewis wrote, 'Everyone says forgiveness is a lovely idea until they have something to forgive.'[8]

So what can we do? As Scripture says, 'Confess your sins to one another, and pray for one another, and this will cure you' (Jas 5:16). The sacrament of reconciliation is a powerful means through which we can bring our faults to the Father of mercies, and hear him stating, through the human voice of the priest, 'I absolve you from your sins'. Knowing that our debt is cancelled by the Cross of Jesus is the starting point, since his love has triumphed over sin and death. We can take comfort from the words of Saint Paul – 'The Lord has forgiven you; now you must do the same' (Col 3:13) – which seem to reverse the order of the *Pater*, but which we can understand as complementing this part of the Lord's Prayer; the Lord has already forgiven us, anticipating our response by doing the same. We also ask Mary, Mother of Mercy, to help us. Letting go of wrongs done to ourselves is one thing, but it may sometimes be harder to forgive cruelty inflicted on those we love. Mary watched as her Son was tortured and put to death (cf. Jn 19:25-7); may she show us how she united her heart with the offering of Jesus, in total acceptance of the Father's will.

We can then consider the martyrs and witnesses to the faith who showed forgiveness to others, often in horrendous circumstances. Whenever I read the verse, 'You are my hiding place, O Lord; you save me from distress' (Ps 31:7), I recall the famous book *The Hiding Place* by Corrie ten Boom (1892–1983), whose Dutch watchmaking family expressed their Christian faith by hiding Jews from the Nazis in their shop premises during World War II.[9] Corrie not only somehow survived a concentration camp, but found the strength to meet with and forgive two of the guards who had been so cruel to her and her sister, who had died in the camp. Corrie insisted in her book (and in her public speaking, sharing the Gospel in over sixty countries for the rest of her life) that only with God's help can we forgive. The title of her book consists of a clever double-meaning: the hiding place is the family shop where their Jewish friends took refuge from persecution, yet the real hiding place is in the heart of God (as above, cf. also Ps 30:21).

What's your dream?

You may have heard the (surely apocryphal) story of the priest who was asked on his ordination day, 'What's your dream, your goal?' His reply was forthright: 'I'm going to convert the whole world!' He was reminded of this at his silver jubilee, as, slightly embarrassed, he stated with a smile, 'If I could just convert my parish ...' Fast-forward another twenty-five years to his golden jubilee; our priest, an old man now, sighed deeply and murmured: 'If I could only convert myself!' Is this downsizing of ambition or sacred realism? Well, it's the realisation that to change the world, we need to change ourselves. You don't have to be a Christian to acknowledge this; yet Christian solidarity implies that when we strive to change, to become what God meant us to be from all eternity – in other words, to become saints – our life and prayer can have immense effect upon others, causing shoots of new life to blossom in the most unlikely places; a kind of 'sacred butterfly effect'.[10] The starting-point for 'converting myself' is surely to believe I am loved and forgiven; I have the awesome dignity of being called a child of the Father, so the more I strive to live in a way which corresponds to this reality, the more I can affirm his merciful love which sets me free, and begin a path to forgiving others as I have been forgiven myself.

Saint John Paul II constantly affirmed the need for personal holiness in order to bring about a better world; the explicit forgiveness he offered to the man who shot him in St Peter's Square in 1981 (causing health issues which would affect the Pope for the rest of his life) reminds us of the healing power found in a simple gesture of reconciliation, and inspires us to believe that even in the most painful experiences of life, God can enable us to go beyond hurt to find peace.

> Forgiveness is above all a personal choice, a decision of the heart to go against the natural instinct to pay back evil with evil. The measure of such a decision is the love of God who draws us to himself in spite of our sin. It has its perfect exemplar in the forgiveness of Christ, who on the Cross prayed: 'Father, forgive them; for they know not what they do.' (Lk 23:34)[11]

7.

Going into Battle

And lead us not into temptation,
but deliver us from evil

The Lord loves those who hate evil: he guards the souls
of his saints.

Psalms 96:10

Our pilgrim life here on earth cannot be without
temptation for it is through temptation that we make
progress and it is only by being tempted that we come to
know ourselves.

Saint Augustine

Testing times

The final two clauses of the Lord's Prayer seem to belong together,
given that through them we ask our heavenly Father to protect us
from temptation and evil; we are thus reminded of the reality of
spiritual warfare: our earthly life is one of battle against 'the world,
the flesh and the devil' (traditionally, the three enemies of the soul).
Whenever Christians – particularly pastors and preachers – are

tempted to coast along blandly proposing a pseudo-gospel of universal niceness, we need to be challenged by the Lord's own words, and reminded that this is the prayer he taught us. Praying the Our Father isn't simply a nice option; for the baptised, it is a command, a mission and a lifeline!

After having requested the food we need each day (and, indeed, the Bread of heaven) and begging forgiveness from the one who calls us to be reconciled with him and with our fellow pilgrims on the journey, we reach the concluding phrase of our prayer. But what does this mean exactly, 'lead us not into temptation'? These words have been much in the news in recent years, due to modifications of both French and Italian versions.[1] A Pentecostal friend asked me anxiously if we Catholics were planning to change our English translation. I replied that this was most unlikely: it's a miracle of divine grace that we have an English version of the Lord's Prayer that all Christians are able to recite together!

According to the Catechism, 'the Greek means both "do not allow us to enter into temptation" and "do not let us yield to temptation".'[2] It should be noted, however, that the key word here (Greek *peirasmos*, Latin *tentatio*) can be rendered by 'temptation', but also by 'trial' and 'test' – which widens the scope of the prayer considerably. The Greek word *peirasmos* is at the origin of our English word 'experience'; I recall a priest I knew who would regularly pray: 'Lord, protect our young people from the dangers of drugs, alcohol and negative affective experiences.' So, deep down, we are pleading with the Father not to put us to the test or allow us to experience a time of trial.

As with every clause of the Lord's Prayer, we must focus on Jesus in order to deepen our understanding of its meaning and claim its power. We know that Jesus was tempted; he 'was led by the Spirit out into the wilderness to be tempted by the devil' (Mt 4:1). Basically, there are three types of temptation: to pride, selfishness and power.[3] Jesus counteracts them with prayer (against pride), penance (against selfishness) and charity (against power) – which are the three tools of spiritual warfare we particularly focus on during Lent (but which, of course, need to be employed throughout the year). They correspond to the three dimensions of our relationships: with God (prayer), with self (penance, confronting our addictions) and with our neighbour (charity). Jesus appears in the Gospels as the new Moses, preparing for his public mission by spending forty days in the wilderness. He defeats the tempter with the power of the Word of God, and reminds us that his help is near in every one of our trials.

We read in the Letter to the Hebrews: 'For it is not as if we had a high priest who was incapable of feeling our weaknesses with us; but we have one who has been tempted in every way that we are, though he is without sin' (4:15). A clarification is required here: Jesus didn't have our disordered desires and was incapable of sin. The second part of the verse could be better rendered: 'We have one who has been tested in every way that we are, yet was sinless.' Above all, we can affirm that, as with everything he did on earth, the Lord underwent this testing *for us and for our salvation*; he shows us how to overcome the suggestions of the evil one, and reminds us that he is with us always (cf. Mt 28:20). We must also be aware of the *eschatological aspect* of this supplication, how it pertains to the end times (and, for the individual believer, our own last day on earth). An alternative rendering of 'lead us not into temptation' would therefore be: *protect us during the time of final testing*, as we implore God's protection to withstand the last trial the Church must pass through before the second coming of Christ (see CCC, 675).

My head you have anointed

The bottom line is that since I'm the Father's beloved child, he's not going to leave me in the lurch; we may feel overwhelmed sometimes by the trials of life and our own failures, but when we look at life with the eyes of faith, we grasp even in a small

way how much he has been protecting us. It's true, we can take
God's presence for granted; how many times are we spared grief
and disaster, even when we are blissfully unaware of his protecting
hand? We can be oblivious to the spiritual battle in the world
and in our own lives; we need to 'put God's armour on so as to
be able to resist the devil's tactics' (Eph 6:11). Simply by striving
to live the Christian life, being as faithful as we can to prayer, the
sacraments and the service of others, we are more protected than
we know. And at moments of great stress we can call out to the
one who will never leave us, or to his friends the saints – they
are rooting for us, having undergone all kinds of tribulations just
like us. A friend told me about a young woman he knew (whose
father had recently died) travelling in the Far East. One evening,
it was getting dark and she sensed an atmosphere of danger. All
she could think of was to call on her late father: 'Dad, help me!'
Immediately, a figure appeared in the dimly lit street: it was one of
her father's best friends, unaccountably visiting the same far-away
place. He at once calmed her fears and brought her safely to her
hotel. Invariably, crying out to God (or his friends) at times of
crisis brings peace. I met a man in Ireland who had once started a
riot in prison; being in a very dark place in his cell, tempted to end
it all, he fell to his knees and cried out to God – and at once felt
the Lord's presence. Then he found his mission, to tell his fellow
prisoners about Jesus (the poor men had no means of escape!) and,
upon his release, worked to bring the Gospel to those who feel
most abandoned by society.

In this final petition of the Lord's Prayer, we are specifically invited
to ask the Father to deliver us from evil (or from the evil one). God
doesn't want us to become fixated with evil or the devil, but to be on
our guard; as Saint Paul said, 'we will not be outwitted by Satan – we
know well enough what his intentions are' (2 Cor 2:11). Our role as
the Father's children in this fragile world is not to be overwhelmed by
evil but to point to signs of his presence and victory.

We all know the psalm 'The Lord is my shepherd'. Full disclosure: the only time I was asked to tend a flock of (two) sheep, they escaped, so I can't claim any expertise in the art of shepherding! Not long ago, my attention was drawn to an interesting interpretation of the verse, 'My head you have anointed with oil' (Ps 22:5). Apparently, sheep are sometimes tormented by flies which lay eggs in their nostrils (which turn into worms), forcing the poor sheep to beat their heads against a rock. But when the shepherd pours oil over the head of the sheep, the oil acts as a screen, thus protecting them from these terrible insects. There's a spiritual parallel for all of us: when we feel tormented by all kinds of trials, negative thoughts and the evil one's insinuations, we can revisit the anointing we have received from the Good Shepherd, and we are safe.

But what can we do? This query is often made by parents, anguished at the dark influences their children are subjected to – whether at school, by peer pressure or the all-invasive forms of media – and it has to be said, there's no easy answer. However, our mere efforts to live our faith and carry out what the Church offers us mean that we enjoy the Lord's protection in a powerful way, for ourselves, our nearest and dearest and surely for many others. If every Catholic prioritised Sunday Mass, daily prayer and regular confession, as well as helping the poor and seeking to evangelise, the world would be transformed! I'm blessed to serve in a dynamic, relatively youthful parish with significant lay participation and strong Mass attendance (even in pandemic times), yet I often reflect on the fact that barely five per cent of my town's population attends a Christian service each week. Not that we're better than the others, but we're called to be signs of God's loving presence for a society which has forgotten him. How would we cope if *everyone* suddenly came to Mass? We'll worry about that when the time comes.

The devil has no knees

A feature of our first holy communion programme is a tour of the church, which includes an explanation about various 'postures' in the liturgy: why we stand, sit or kneel at different moments during Mass. Once I mentioned casually to the wide-eyed children that long ago a monk had a vision of the devil in his cell, and *the devil had no knees!*[4] The point being that he refuses to (or cannot) kneel in adoration before the one God. A wise Glaswegian mum whispers as we move on, 'You realise, Father, that's the only thing they'll remember from your talk!' Without wishing to make those who can't kneel for health reasons feel at all guilty, it's good to be mindful of the positive aspect of bowing down or kneeling before the one who created us for relationship with him, and to worship him as he deserves. We can also surmise that the Father has knees: like a good dad, he takes us on his knee to hug us and tell us that all will be well, and that he will never leave us, since we are his beloved offspring.

It's important to affirm that calmly reciting 'deliver us from evil' is a powerful means of protection from dark spiritual forces: when said with faith, it truly is a deliverance prayer! We must distinguish *exorcism* (as an extraordinary rite of the Church, used only by priests and then only in extreme cases) from *deliverance ministry*, which 'should be a normal part of evangelisation, even of the sacrament of Reconciliation'.[5] If we live in the name of Jesus, we can call upon his power to protect us from all the attacks of the evil one, at any time.

Once upon a time

I stood outside the impressive Anglican Church of St Mary in North Petherton, Somerset (sadly closed at the time due to the Covid-19 pandemic), with much to reflect on. It was here that my (deep breath) great-great-great-great-great-great-great-great grandparents Henry Woollond and Joan Porter were married in 1611 (incidentally, the same year in which the King James Bible was published in English and Hatfield House in Hertfordshire opened).[6] The family stayed in the area for quite a while: their great-great grandson Henry Wollen married Grace Dinnis in 1779, in the same church. A moment like this gives rise to numerous philosophical questions, mostly starting with 'What if … ?' – not to mention a consideration of how the spelling of surnames can evolve over the years! I calculate that I would have had just over a thousand 'eight times great' grandparents. Factor in all the siblings at each stage, with their spouses and extended families: there's quite a crowd in each family tree. So many love stories, joys and sorrows, so much heartbreak and tragedy make up the history of each family; how many encounters and providential circumstances had to happen for each of us to come into existence at all!

The believer can see the hand of God at work through the generations, knowing that 'before the world was made, God chose us in Christ, to be holy and spotless, and to live through love in his presence' (Eph 1:4). The family tree of Jesus himself is our template, particularly as narrated at the beginning of Matthew's Gospel: 'Abraham was the father of Isaac, Isaac the father of Jacob …' (Mt 1:2) – never the easiest Gospel reading to proclaim in the liturgy, even if it appears only a couple of times a year! These verses provide us with the merest glimpse of how the Father works through the ups and downs of human history to bring about the birth of the Messiah. After some forty generations, we reach the culminating point with a certain relief: 'Jacob was the father of Joseph the husband of Mary; of her was born Jesus who is called Christ' (1:16) – the centuries-long awaiting for the Holy One of the Lord is finally over.

Yes, Jesus himself had quite a complicated family history (even if we allow that Joseph was his foster-father). If we research just those names in Joseph's line that are mentioned in the Old Testament, we find plenty of colourful material, good and evil, sin and shame, grief and heartbreak. Yet this was how God worked through the often dysfunctional character of human activity to bring about the fulfilment of his plan: 'When the appointed time came, God sent his Son, born of a woman, born a subject of the Law, to redeem the subjects of the Law and to enable us to be adopted as sons' (Gal 4:4). I'm somewhat wary of some of the tenets of a contemporary Christian movement devoted to 'healing the family tree', particularly the concept that the evils people suffer today (whether psychological, spiritual or physical) have a cause in their ancestors.[7] The Church simply invites us to pray for the souls of our deceased ancestors and loved ones, entrusting them to the mercy of God.[8]

Good times

The Christian message is that good triumphs over evil, yet God permits bad things in order to bring about a greater good; we see this above all in the Cross of Jesus, the greatest evil ever perpetrated in history – the elimination of the eternal Son of God born into our world, who came to save his people – yet the very means by which this salvation is accomplished. 'Jesus was to die for the nation – and not for the nation only, but to gather together in unity the scattered children of God' (Jn 11:51-2). Benedict XVI writes movingly about the silence of God in the face of human trial:

> Often we cannot understand why God refrains from intervening. Yet he does not prevent us from crying out, like Jesus on the Cross: 'My God, my God, why have you forsaken me?' (Mt 27:46) Our crying out is, as it was for Jesus on the Cross, the deepest and most radical way of affirming our faith in his sovereign power. Even in their bewilderment and failure to understand the world around them, Christians continue to believe in the 'goodness and loving kindness of God' (Ti 3:4). Immersed like everyone else in the dramatic complexity of historical events, they

remain unshakably certain that God is our Father and loves us, even when his silence remains incomprehensible.[9]

We all love tales which show God's plan working through and despite human failings and hardship; we can cite, for example, the life story of Francis George (1937–2015) who contracted polio at the age of thirteen. He wanted to be a priest, but was rejected by the minor seminary of the Archdiocese of Chicago due to his condition. Persevering, he was accepted by a religious order, the Oblates of Mary Immaculate, and was eventually ordained. Many years later, after being chosen to serve as a bishop in Washington and Oregon states, he was appointed Archbishop (later Cardinal) of Chicago! One presumes that whoever rejected him for his native diocese nearly fifty years earlier had already gone to God.

As mentioned in chapter 2, Psalm 90 is particularly recommended to invoke God's protection – not least in a time of pandemic: 'Upon you no evil shall fall, no plague approach where you dwell. For you has he commanded his angels, to keep you in all your ways' (vv. 10-11). The Lord thus reminds us of the presence of his *angels* at our side in all our troubles, for they have a mission to keep his children from harm and guide us ever closer to the kingdom. 'From infancy to death human life is surrounded by their watchful care and intercession. "Beside each believer stands an angel as protector and shepherd leading him to life." Already here on earth the Christian life shares by faith in the blessed company of angels and men united in God.'[10] The quite mysterious book of Tobit in the Old Testament describes how the Archangel Raphael (whose name means *God's healing*) protects Tobias and his wife Sarah, and directs Tobias to heal his father Tobit's blindness (with ointment) before revealing his identity: 'I am Raphael, one of the seven angels who stand ever ready to enter the presence of the glory of the Lord … Now bless the Lord on earth and give thanks to God' (Tob 12:15, 20).

Healing and strength for the final journey

It seems appropriate that the sacrament of the anointing of the sick should be associated with this final clause of the Lord's Prayer. 'If one of you is ill, he should send for the elders of the church, and they must anoint him with oil in the name of the Lord and pray over him' (Jas 5:14). My golden rule for praying with someone in a coma or who is unresponsive is to assume they can hear everything, which was confirmed recently in a local hospital: I anointed an apparently unresponsive patient, without any immediate reaction. When I'd finished the prayers, however, he slowly moved his arm in a clear attempt to make the Sign of the Cross, a sight moving to behold. Beyond any physical change, this sacrament certainly brings inner healing and strength for the final journey. Anticipating this healing, we confidently make our desires known to the Saviour, with the help of St Paul's beautiful prayer:

> This, then, is what I pray, kneeling before the Father, from whom every family, whether spiritual or natural, takes its name: Out of his infinite glory, may he give you the power through his Spirit for your hidden self to grow strong, so that Christ may live in your hearts through faith, and then, planted in love and built on love, you will with all the saints have strength to grasp the breadth and the length, the height and the depth; until, knowing the love of Christ, which is beyond all knowledge, you are filled with the utter fullness of God. (Eph 3:14-19)

May the Lord deliver us from all danger, heal us of all that impedes us on our path, and open up the way to life with him. May our Blessed Mother Mary, the woman 'adorned with the sun' (Rv 12:1), take our side in our battle against the dragon, and guide us ever closer to her Son, who underwent all kinds of trials for us and for our salvation, until we reach the Father's kingdom of light and love.

Postscript
In the Heart of the Father

The sun is shining

It's a hot and sunny June day in Tiberias. Some people are swimming in the warm water of the Sea of Galilee, others are sunning themselves on the beach. I see a small child running to his dad, shouting: 'Abba! Abba!' I reflect on the extraordinary effort made by the Israelis who somehow managed, against all the odds, to revive their ancient biblical tongue as a modern language; then I think about how this little boy relates to his father, laughing and playing by the water as children do. There are no worries, the sun is shining; the child is safe and feels loved, valued, because his daddy cares for him and even wants to play with him. This is how it should be for every family, of course. And since the Christian family is called to image the life and love at the heart of the Holy Trinity, then family matters.

It's an evidence that these are difficult times for families; all of us see the most heart-wrenching situations around us and in society. Without claiming to propose solutions, a starting point for helping towards healing family life is for each of us Christians to *live more fully our vocation as children of God* – and the simple yet profound prayer of the Our Father is our template, our guide and our gateway to paradise. If we are already children of God through baptism, we ask the Lord to help us *become more and more what we are* – and so witness to others that they too are called and chosen to be the Father's children.

> Of course, our being children of God does not have the fullness of Jesus. We must increasingly become so throughout the journey of our Christian existence, developing in the following of Christ and in communion with him so as to enter ever more intimately into the relationship of love with God the Father which sustains our life. It is this fundamental reality that is disclosed to us when we open ourselves to the Holy Spirit and he makes us turn to God saying 'Abba', Father. We have truly preceded creation, entering into adoption with Jesus; united, we are really in God and are his children in a new way, in a new dimension.[1]

As believers, we can sometimes feel downhearted when faced with our own limitations, our failure to reflect the Father's love for the world. When Jesus states, 'You must call no one on earth your father' (Mt 23:9), he surely means that we cannot image the Father's goodness unless we have at least the desire to become like him.[2] If we asked the Lord what to do about our apparent inability to progress in the spiritual life, he might reply 'I'm working on it!', or words to that effect. The more we experience our sinful state, the more we can grow in trust in his mercy. 'Intercessor, friend of sinners, earth's Redeemer, plead for me, where the songs of all the sinless sweep across the crystal sea.'[3]

The hope that springs eternal
Galway City, on the west coast of Ireland, is a magnet for artists, tourists and 'alternative lifestyle seekers'. It is less well-known for its unlikely role in initiating a worldwide movement which

has brought untold blessings to the Church over the past forty years. When St John Paul II visited Ireland in 1979, less than a year after his election, he presided over a large gathering for young people at Ballybrit racecourse outside Galway City. There are strong suggestions that this enthusiastic encounter, possibly his first youth event as pope, gave John Paul the idea of the World Youth Days, which take place every two or three years, in different parts of the world. If you've experienced the exhausting, yet exhilarating adventure of 'WYDs', you'll know they bring many blessings to the young (and older!) participants, and sow the seeds of countless vocations; to priesthood, religious life and Christian marriage. Sometimes God enables us to witness to his grace in unexpected ways. During one of the World Youth Days, a priest friend from another group passing by asked me to hear his confession (which I did), then I asked him to hear mine. On the way back, everyone was sharing stories; I asked the young people from my group what had most touched them about their experience. One girl said her most memorable moment was seeing two priests hearing each other's confessions: she'd never seen anything like it!

John Paul II memorably proclaimed at the World Youth Day in Canada:

> Although I have lived through much darkness, under harsh totalitarian regimes, I have seen enough evidence to be unshakeably convinced that no difficulty, no fear is so great that it can completely suffocate the hope that springs eternal in the hearts of the young … Do not let that hope die! Stake your lives on it! We are not the sum of our weaknesses and failures; we are the sum of the Father's love for us and our real capacity to become the image of his Son.[4]

We are not the sum of our weaknesses and failures; we are the sum of the Father's love for us!

Reading once more the 'priestly prayer of Christ' in chapter 17 of John's Gospel, which echoes the Lord's Prayer in several ways, we find a sort of summary of the mission of Jesus in the final verse (26): 'I have made your name known to them and will continue to make it known, so that the love with which you loved me may be in them, and so that I may be in them.' If we believe that the Father cannot refuse any prayer of his beloved Son, we can affirm that this love of the Father will eventually spread through the Church to the whole world, and will be celebrated in all the faithful for eternity!⁵

Amen to that

When you walk along a paved road, you generally proceed with confidence, trusting that the ground beneath will not fail you. A friend who had experienced a major earthquake (in California) described it as the most terrifying event she'd ever been through. It's hard to imagine how one would react if faced with such an ordeal. Asphalt is something we often take for granted – and it's in the Bible! At least, the Greek origin of the word, meaning firmness or dependability, is found, for example, at the very beginning of Luke's Gospel: 'I ... have decided to write an ordered account for you, Theophilus, so that your Excellency may learn how well founded the teaching is that you have received' (Lk 1:3-4). The word translated as 'well founded', *asphalia*, also suggests assurance, reliability, certainty.⁶

Everyone yearns for something reliable, dependable; as solid as the road they walk on. In fact, all people have a deep-seated craving for *truth*, even if they are unaware of this or refute the very concept. We tend to think of truth as something static; a list of facts or dogmas to be learned. When we begin to make the Lord's word our home (cf. Jn 8:31-2) – finding shelter therein from the storms of life – we encounter the truth first of all as a person, Jesus himself who is the Truth, and we discover the truth that we are loved and called to love. In the book of the Apocalypse, Jesus is described as 'the Amen, the faithful, the true witness' (Rv 3:14). Saint Paul echoes this, speaking of Jesus as Son of God: 'however many the promises God made, the Yes to them all is in him [Jesus]. That is why it is "through him" that we answer Amen to the praise of God' (2 Cor 1:20).

Therefore, whenever we say this little word 'Amen' we are giving our Yes to God's plan for our lives, responding to his invitation and welcoming all his saving promises made to us through his Son.[7] We join our willingness to serve to that of Mary at her Annunciation (cf. Lk 1:38) and of all the saints and people of good will throughout history. We journey along a way that is sure and dependable, because Jesus himself is the Way to the Father. He is Truth, so he will realise all the Father's beautiful plans for us if we let him; and he is Life, calling us to share in the eternal life he willed for us before time began (cf. Jn 14:6; Eph 1:4). Jewish tradition states that in a certain fashion, the person who responds Amen is even greater than the one who pronounces the blessing and that saying Amen with proper concentration has the power to open the gates of the Garden of Eden and nullify negative decrees.[8] Remember that the next time you're at Mass! One key psalm verse could be called the ultimate happy ending: 'You will show me the path of life, the fullness of joy in your presence, at your right hand happiness for ever' (Ps 15:11). Once we grasp that Jesus himself is the pathway, we can claim the joy of God's presence through his Holy Spirit, as we await the fullness of life in heaven. We may not experience this happiness right now, but we can keep going with confidence, trusting that the happiness we don't yet feel is stored up for us in the next world.

Finding healing in the Lord's Prayer

As mentioned previously, reciting one Our Father usually takes about twenty seconds. However, the benefits of taking more time over this prayer are immense and immeasurable! It goes without saying that the more attuned we are to the divine ways, the more we will find blessings in this, and every kind of prayer. It's said that once an actor and a farmhand were asked to recite the Lord's Prayer in turn at a harvest festival. Afterwards, the actor remarked, 'I knew the words, but he knew the author'.

To get to 'know the author', we need to spend time with him. There are many ways of praying, but one of the simplest and most effective is surely to dwell on the Lord's Prayer – as I've personally discovered in a new way while writing this book. If we begin by picturing ourselves being tenderly held in the Father's hand (or call to mind a similar image we feel to be appropriate), then we start: *Our Father, who art in heaven* – and stop there! Remain in silence with that first line; think about the Father, or about heaven, or one of the themes of our first chapter, such as the wonderful gift of being called a child of God through baptism. After ten, twenty, thirty seconds of silence, we go on to the next line: *Hallowed be thy name.* And so on. Now we don't have to feel we should be like mystics who could spend an hour over this one prayer, but we can presume that time spent dwelling on the words our Saviour gave us is never time wasted. Meditating the *Pater* line by line can draw us into a closer relationship with its author, unleashing great graces of healing and peace for ourselves and those we love. In addition, we will become vessels of divine help for others, thus fulfilling our baptismal calling to be messengers of the good news for a culture seeking meaning and hope:

> God desires his children to bring his mercy to the world, operating in the full range of charisms and the supernatural

power of the Holy Spirit. If we give the Lord permission to do all that he desires to do in us, he will use us to minister his healing power to the sick and the suffering, revealing his love and the presence of his glorious kingdom.[9]

Healing has been a kind of conducting thread throughout our reading of the Lord's Prayer; the good news is the Lord wants to make us whole. We read in the Catechism an affirmation of the *more radical healing* Jesus has in store for each one of us:

> Moved by so much suffering Christ not only allows himself to be touched by the sick, but he makes their miseries his own: 'He took our infirmities and bore our diseases.' But he did not heal all the sick. His healings were signs of the coming of the Kingdom of God. They announced a more radical healing: the victory over sin and death through his Passover. By his passion and death on the cross Christ has given a new meaning to suffering: it can henceforth configure us to him and unite us with his redemptive Passion.[10]

With a father's heart: Saint Joseph

I've written elsewhere about Saint Joseph as an icon of the Father.[11] The providential timing of Pope Francis' Apostolic Letter *Patris Corde* nudges me to conclude by turning once more to this great saint as a model for our times and an encouraging witness to the Father's loving-kindness:

> In every exercise of our fatherhood, we should always keep in mind that it has nothing to do with possession, but is rather a 'sign' pointing to a greater fatherhood. In a way, we are all like Joseph: a shadow of the heavenly Father, who 'makes his sun rise on the evil and on the good, and

sends rain on the just and on the unjust'. And a shadow that follows his Son.'[12]

If we find that God is too remote, too removed from our daily struggle, if the wounds suffered at the hands of authority figures seem to paralyse us or prevent us from approaching God as a loving parent, we can 'go to Joseph' (Gn 41:55) to encounter a fatherly heart encouraging us to trust in God and grow in understanding for the weaknesses of others, until we too learn to become *merciful like the Father* (cf. Lk 6:36). May Joseph and Mary continue to intercede for all God's children, helping us to put Jesus at the centre of our lives as they did, inviting us to discover by our contemplation of the Saviour, the amazing secret that Jesus shares with his friends: 'To have seen me is to have seen the Father' (Jn 14:9). For the kingdom, the power and the glory are yours, now and for ever. Amen!

Hail, Guardian of the Redeemer,
Spouse of the Blessed Virgin Mary.
To you God entrusted his only Son;
in you Mary placed her trust;
with you Christ became man.

Blessed Joseph, to us too,
show yourself a father
and guide us in the path of life.
Obtain for us grace, mercy and courage,
and defend us from every evil. Amen.[13]

Appendix
The Lord's Prayer and the Sacraments

A. Sacraments to be received only once[1]

1. Baptism
Our Father, who art in heaven

'Think of the love that the Father has lavished on us, by letting us be called God's children, and that is what we are.' (1 Jn 3:1)

2. Priesthood
Hallowed be thy name

'I have made your name known to the men you took from the world to give me. They were yours and you gave them to me, and they have kept your word.' (Jn 17:6)

3. Confirmation
Thy kingdom come

'The kingdom of God does not mean eating or drinking this or that, it means righteousness and peace and joy brought by the Holy Spirit.' (Rm 14:17)

4. **Marriage**
   Thy will be done on earth as it is in heaven
   'Give way to one another in obedience to Christ.'
   (Eph 5:21)

B. Sacraments of healing, to be received more than once[2]

   5. **Eucharist**
      Give us this day our daily bread
      'Anyone who eats this bread will live for ever.' (Jn 6:58)

   6. **Reconciliation**
      And forgive us our trespasses,
      as we forgive those who trespass against us
      'My child, your sins are forgiven.' (Mk 2:5)

   7. **Anointing of the Sick**
      And lead us not into temptation,
      but deliver us from evil
      'The prayer of faith will save the sick man and the Lord
      will raise him up again.' (Jas 5:15)

Author's website: www.nigelwoollen.com

Endnotes

Preface: Mircle Prayer

1   *Liturgy of the Hours*, Office of Readings, Second Reading for 30 July, memorial of the saint.

2   Dale Carnegie, *How to Stop Worrying and Start Living*, Bungay, Suffolk: Richard Clay (The Chaucer Press), 1948, p. 139.

3   CCC, 2763, quoting St Thomas Aquinas, *Summa Theologica*, II-II, 83, 9.

4   CCC, 2777, quoting St Peter Chrysologus, Sermo 71, 3.

5   *Liturgy of the Hours*, Office of Readings, Second Reading for 17 October, memorial of the saint.

6   The same prayer also occurs in a shorter form in Luke 11:2-4, which will not be examined in this study, except for an interesting textual variant (see chapter 3).

7   Rev. Alfred Marshall, *The RSV Interlinear Greek-English New Testament*, Basingstoke: Marshall-Pickering, 1968/1975, p. 20. 'Interlinear' means that the nearest English equivalent is placed beneath each Greek word in the New Testament text, thus enabling even someone who has no Greek to get a feel for the original version of the Bible. Marshall's edition is highly recommended, not least for its masterly introduction.

1. We are Family: Our Father, who art in heaven

1   Bangalore: official name Bengaluru, but everyone I met referred to the city by this name.

2   Francis, Address at Croke Park Stadium, Dublin, 25 August 2018.

3   John Henry Newman, *Meditations and Devotions*, London: Longmans, Green & Co., 1907, p. 299. First published 1893.

4   *Gaudium et Spes*, 1.

5   *Gaudium et Spes*, 24.

6   As we shall see later, taking more time over our recitation of the Lord's Prayer can be healing and even life-changing.

7   CCC, 2781.

8   Long before Abba was the name of a Swedish pop group it meant Daddy or Papa in Hebrew. A suggested acronym: Awesome, Benevolent, Beautiful, Adorable. You might like to devise your own.

9   See John XXIII, *Journal of a Soul*, London: Geoffrey Chapman, 1965, p. 17, where he adds a quote from Ecclesiasticus (7:36): 'In everything you do, remember your end, and you will never sin.'

10   CCC, 260.

11   CCC, 2563.

12   The rather daunting command of Jesus, 'Be perfect, just as your heavenly Father is perfect' (Mt 5:48) could also be translated: 'Be whole-hearted, just as your heavenly Father is whole-hearted', a version which helps to shed light on our human idea of 'perfection'. This alternative rendering was proposed by Fr Francis Martin (1930–2017), a widely-respected American Scripture scholar (and family friend).

13   CCC, 2795.

14   One day I was sulking because my team had lost a cup final, then a lady rang to tell me her family home had burnt to the ground (fortunately no one was hurt and the house was rebuilt with the insurance money); sometimes we need to be reminded that our troubles are slight compared to those of other people.

15   Benedict XVI, Homily for the Feast of the Baptism of the Lord, 7 January 2007.

2. Our Real Identity: Hallowed be thy name

1   In Orthodox theology (which describes the event as the 'unburnt bush'), Mary's giving birth to the Saviour without loss of virginity is analogous to the bush burning without being consumed.

2   So named because pilgrims would remove their footwear at this point to walk the Holy Mile into the village.

3   The word 'hallow' comes from Old English *halig*, which has evolved into our modern term 'holy'. The sixteenth century vocabulary of the Lord's Prayer can be challenging; however, most people are familiar with the term 'hallowed ground' which conveys the sense of a sacred place, separate from ordinary use that begs of us an attitude of reverence. (Football fans easily grasp the concept of the 'hallowed turf' of Wembley Stadium,

for example.) The word 'holy' also suggests the notion of wholeness, completeness, which is certainly in tune with the biblical concept.

4   Of course, many people use various given names for different occasions. I'm sure I'm not the only minister ever to preside at a funeral who, after extolling at length the virtues of the deceased (let's call her Agatha), was aghast to hear a relative beginning the eulogy, 'We all loved Belinda …' This concept of using diverse names, common to various cultures, can shed light on certain apparent inconsistencies in names in the Bible.

5   The Greek word used for 'in' here is the dynamic *eis* rather than the more expected *en*, implying movement: we could almost translate the Sign of the Cross thus: *Into* the name of the Father and of the Son and of the Holy Spirit. 'The use of *eis* seems to suggest the end and effect of baptism, a special relation to the Holy Trinity assumed by the person baptised' (*Biblical Greek* by Maximilian Zerwick SJ, Rome: Scripta Pontificii Instituti Biblici, 1963, p. 35).

6   Leo I, Sermon 1 for the Nativity, 2.3.

7   CCC, 2812. Various Bible references here include John 17 and Philippians 2:9-11.

8   The seminal work *Old Testament Priests and the New Priest* (Chicago: Gracewing, 2009) by Albert (later Cardinal) Vanhoye SJ (1923–2021) brings great clarity to the debate about the nature of priesthood in Scripture (originally published in French in 1980).

9   Psalms 91 in the original Hebrew. If by the grace of God I get to heaven, I might want to have a quiet word with the scribe who had the bright idea of merging Psalms 9 and 10 into one when translating the Hebrew Bible into Greek, thus causing confusion over psalm numbering for the following twenty-three centuries.

3. To Serve is to Reign: Thy kingdom come

1   See CCC, 2816.

2   Or 'within you' – an alternative translation.

3   We will consider in more depth in chapter 5 the different ways in which God responds to our prayers of demand.

4   *The Complete Works of Elizabeth of the Trinity*, Vol. 1, Aletheia Kane OCD (trans.), Washington D.C.: ICS Publications, 2014, p. 183, quoting Matthew 17:5. The original French – '*que je lui sois une humanité de surcroît*' - has also been translated: 'that I may be an extra-added humanity'. 'The Prayer was written by her on 21 November 1904, on the day of the feast of the Presentation. The whole community renewed their religious

profession on that day. When she returned to the cell, she took up her pen, and on a common sheet of paper from a notebook without hesitation and without any correction, in one stroke she wrote the prayer. It came spontaneously as an outpouring of the heart.' ('A biblical rereading of the spiritual experience and Vision of Elizabeth of the Trinity' by Augustine Mulloor OCD, *Teresianum* 59: 2008, p. 79, footnote 54.)

5   'Christ has communicated this royal power to his disciples that they might be constituted in royal freedom and that by true penance and a holy life they might conquer the reign of sin in themselves. Further, he has shared this power so that serving Christ in their fellow men they might by humility and patience lead their brethren to that King for whom to serve is to reign' (*Lumen Gentium*, 36).

6   CCC, 1147.

7   Francis, Prayer Vigil with the Young People (World Youth Day), Krakow, 30 July 2016.

8   See, for example, 1 Timothy 2:5, John 5:26-27 and 2 Timothy 4:1 (reprised in both the Niceno-Constantinopolitan and Apostles' Creeds).

9   'Believing is an act of the intellect assenting to the divine truth by command of the will moved by God through grace' (CCC, 155, quoting Saint Thomas Aquinas). We could probably spend a lifetime meditating on this one sentence!

10   Bruce M. Metzger, *Textual Commentary on the Greek New Testament*, Stuttgart: Deutsche Bibelgesellschaft, 1994, p. 131: 'Apparently … the variant reading is a liturgical adaptation of the original form of the Lord's Prayer, used perhaps when celebrating the rite of baptism or the laying on of hands.'

11   CCC, 2818–9.

12   Archpriest Maxim Nikolsky (ed.), *The Aim of Christian Life: The Conversation of St Seraphim of Sarov with N. A. Motovilov*, Cambridge: Saints Alive Press, 2010.

13   The traditional masculine pronouns (he, him) for the Holy Spirit may be problematic for some readers. Interestingly, the word for spirit or breath is masculine in Latin (*spiritus*), neuter in Greek (*pneuma*) and feminine in Hebrew (*ruah*)!

14   CCC, 567. The Catechism also refers here to a magnificent passage (5) of *Lumen Gentium*, the Dogmatic Constitution on the Church of Vatican II: 'When Jesus, who had suffered the death of the cross for mankind, had risen, he appeared as the one constituted as Lord, Christ and eternal Priest, (cf. Acts 2:36; Heb 5:6; 7:17-21) and he poured out on his disciples the Spirit promised by the Father (cf. Acts 2:33). From this source the

Church, equipped with the gifts of its Founder and faithfully guarding his precepts of charity, humility and self-sacrifice, receives the mission to proclaim and to spread among all peoples the Kingdom of Christ and of God and to be, on earth, the initial budding forth of that kingdom. While it slowly grows, the Church strains toward the completed Kingdom and, with all its strength, hopes and desires to be united in glory with its King.'

4. From Prodigal to Redeemed: Thy will be done on earth as it is in heaven

1   *Le courage d'avoir peur* by the late French Dominican Fr Marie-Dominique Molinié, Paris: Cerf, 1994, sadly not translated into English.

2   CCC, 2826, with reference to Romans 12:2.

3   An alphabetical list of the key words found in the Bible, often included at the end of study Bibles.

4   Variously attributed to Saint Teresa of Ávila and Saint Thérèse of Lisieux, though most likely attributable to English poet Minnie Louise Haskins (1875–1957) in her collection *The Desert* (published privately, 1902).

5   'Wouldn't It Be Nice' by the Beach Boys (1966: Capitol): yet at the culminant point of the lyrical idea, the chord change seems to underline the irony implicit in the statement.

6   CCC, 2827. The theme of *covenant* is central here once more: "'Christ loved the Church and gave himself up for her, that he might sanctify her" (Eph 5:25-6). He has joined her with himself in an everlasting covenant and never stops caring for her as for his own body' (CCC, 796).

7   From a letter written in August 1901, *Lettres à Henry de Castries*, Paris: Grasset, 1938, p. 95–8. English-language version from CatholicSaints.info: https://catholicsaints.info/saint-charles-de-foucauld; accessed on 28 March 2022.

8   Written in his early years as a Trappist, part of a long meditation on the passion of Jesus. English-language version from Charlesdefoucauld.org: https://www.charlesdefoucauld.org/en/priere.php?id_trad=20; accessed on 28 March 2022.

9   French, German, Italian, Spanish, Portuguese, Dutch, Swedish, Hebrew, Irish, Lithuanian, Polish and Croatian. Many of these languages follow the word order of New Testament Greek: 'as in heaven also on earth'. The Latin version of the *Missale Romanum* also follows the Greek word order, with two commas – '*fiat voluntas tua, sicut in cælo, et in terra*' – while Filipino (Tagalog) pauses after both 'done' and 'earth'. As for Russian,

several different versions were found; that used in Catholic circles has a comma after 'earth'. In passing, the polyphonic version of the Lord's Prayer in Russian (*Otche nash*) by Nikolai Kedrov Sr (easily found online, also in English translation) is surely one of the most moving short pieces of choral music ever composed.

5. You are What You Eat: Give us this day our daily bread

1   CCC, 2828.

2   *Liturgy of the Hours*, Office of Readings, Second Reading for Saturday of week 32 in Ordinary Time.

3   Francis-Xarier Nguyên Van Thuân, *Testimony to Hope*, Rome: Pauline Books, 2000, p. 131 – his book born of those small calendar pages, a challenge to us authors with our laptops and creature comforts!

4   CCC, 2833: "'Our' bread is the "one" loaf for the "many". In the Beatitudes "poverty" is the virtue of sharing: it calls us to communicate and share both material and spiritual goods, not by coercion but out of love, so that the abundance of some may remedy the needs of others' (with reference to 2 Cor 8:1-15).

5   I was once the guest preacher at a Sunday Mass, in a context which was a diplomatic minefield, one might say. On the Saturday, I thought nervously that I'd better take a look at the Gospel of the Sunday to prepare something to say; it was this very passage from Matthew: 'Do not worry about tomorrow' – I'm not sure if this meant I wasn't to bother preparing a homily, but reading it affirmed God's gentle humour ... and all went well.

6   Francis, *Patris Corde*, 2.

7   As well as praising this small boy for his offering, we should also acknowledge his mum or dad who presumably made his packed lunch! Could they have suspected, in preparing his snack that morning, that a simple, everyday gesture would have such life-giving consequences?

8   This is the central theme of the best-selling book *Prison to Praise* by Merlin Carothers (London: Hodder & Stoughton, 1970), which has inspired so many Christians over the years. There is a distinction between praising God 'in' all things and 'for' all things – but they can be understood as equivalent if we distinguish (once more) God's *positive* will from his *permissive* will.

9   *Roman Missal*, The Order of Mass, 137, Priest's private prayer after holy communion.

10   *Liturgy of the Hours*, Feast of Corpus Christi, Antiphon for Evening Prayer.

11   Blessed Carlo was Italian but born in London and baptised in the striking
      Servite parish church of Our Lady of Dolours, Chelsea. In my previous
      book *Learning to Love: Journeys through Life with the Rosary* (Dublin:
      Veritas, 2018), I cited Blessed Chiara Badano (1971–90) as possibly
      the first person born after me already beatified (p. 140); Carlo has since
      broken all the records!

12   'In Mary most holy, we also see perfectly fulfilled the "sacramental" way
      that God comes down to meet his creatures and involves them in his
      saving work. … Every time we approach the Body and Blood of Christ in
      the eucharistic liturgy, we also turn to her who, by her complete fidelity,
      received Christ's sacrifice for the whole Church. She is the *Immaculata*,
      who receives God's gift unconditionally and is thus associated with his
      work of salvation. Mary of Nazareth, icon of the nascent Church, is the
      model for each of us, called to receive the gift that Jesus makes of himself
      in the Eucharist.' (Benedict XVI, *Sacramentum Caritatis*, 22 February
      2007, no. 33)

13   Saint Leo the Great seems to think so: 'As they ate with him, their eyes
      were opened in the breaking of bread – opened much more happily to the
      revealed glory of our nature than were the eyes of the first members of our
      race who were filled with shame at their sin' (Sermon 1 on the Ascension
      – 2).

6. Your Sins are Forgiven: And forgive us our trespasses, as we forgive those who trespass against us

1   In a world of so many Bible versions, I've often found that God can
      speak to us in different ways through various translations according to
      our needs at a specific time.

2   In Mark's version, they simply 'stripped the roof' whereas Luke (5:19)
      describes how the friends 'lowered him and his stretcher down through
      the tiles'. Most commentaries assume Luke has adapted his tale for his
      readers of the Hellenistic world; but who knows, maybe some wealthy,
      eccentric person who was much travelled, had decided to place tiles on
      the roof of this house in Capernaum.

3   See Haggai 2:10-14 on a question to the priests concerning ritual purity.

4   The following verse reads: 'Blasphemy against the Spirit will not be
      forgiven' – understood by many theologians to imply definitive rejection
      of God's mercy; God can forgive everything except the person who
      refuses his forgiveness.

5   CCC, 2838. We can also note that the Greek word (in most manuscripts) for 'as we forgive' is in the past tense, so it could be translated: 'Forgive us our trespasses as we *have forgiven* those who trespass against us', making the requirement to forgive others before we seek God's clemency more explicit – 'unless it represents a Semitic perfect which in certain circumstances may have [the] present tense' (Max Zerwick SJ and Mary Grosvenor, *A Grammatical Analysis of the Greek New Testament*, Rome: Editrice Pontificio Istituto Biblico, 1988, p. 16).

6   'Love one another, as I have loved you' (Jn 13:34); 'Be compassionate as your Father is compassionate' (Lk 6:36); 'Be perfect as your heavenly Father is perfect' (Mt 5:48).

7   'It is not in our power not to feel or to forget an offence; but the heart that offers itself to the Holy Spirit turns injury into compassion and purifies the memory in transforming the hurt into intercession.' (CCC, 2843, with reference to this parable in Matthew 18).

8   C.S. Lewis, *Mere Christianity*, New York: MacMillan, 1952, p. 115.

9   Corrie ten Boom with John and Elizabeth Sherill, *The Hiding Place* London: Hodder & Stoughton, 2004.

10   The 'butterfly effect', the theory that a tornado could find its causation in the beating of a butterfly's wings some weeks previously, can certainly be applied to the spiritual life.

11   John Paul II, Message for World Day of Peace, 1 January 2002.

7. Going into Battle: And lead us not into temptation, but deliver us from evil

1   French: previously '*ne nous soumets pas à la tentation*' ('do not subject us to temptation') was changed to '*ne nous laisse pas entrer en tentation*' ('do not allow us to enter into temptation') in the Catholic liturgy in 2017; the new translation has been generally welcomed, as many people were unhappy with the previous one, which could be interpreted as implying that God could tempt us in order to make us sin. Italian: previously '*non ci indurre in tentazione*' ('do not induce/bring us into temptation') was modified to '*non abbandonarci alla tentazione*' ('do not abandon us to temptation') by the Italian Bishops' Conference in 2020; however, it does not seem to have been universally adopted (during a global rosary broadcast with Pope Francis in the Vatican gardens during the 2020 pandemic, the old version was used).

2   CCC, 2846.

3   Corresponding to the triple formula of 1 John 2:16: 'the sensual body, the lustful eye, pride in possessions.'

4   'There is a story that comes from the sayings of the Desert Fathers, according to which the devil was compelled by God to show himself to a certain Abba Apollo. He looked ugly, with frighteningly thin limbs, but, most strikingly, *he had no knees*. The inability to kneel is seen as the very essence of the diabolical.' (Joseph Ratzinger [later Benedict XVI], *The Spirit of the Liturgy*, San Francisco: Ignatius Press, 2000, p. 194.) Abba Apollo lived around CE 300.

5   Neal Lozano, *Resisting the Devil: A Catholic Perspective on Deliverance*, Huntingdon, IN: OSV, 2009, p. 15.

6   Grateful thanks to my cousin Martin Weiler for his extensive research into the Woollen family tree, with prayers for the continued success of his beloved Exeter City Football Club.

7   The International Association of Exorcists addressed this issue in September 2018, under the direction of Fr Rogelio Alcántara, who delivered a decidedly negative evaluation of intergenerational healing. See Luis Santamaría, 'Can we "heal our family tree" and wipe out "ancestral sin"?', *Aleteia*, 2 December 2018. https://aleteia.org/2018/12/02/can-we-heal-our-family-tree-and-wipe-out-ancestral-sin; accessed on 27 February 2021.

8   A foundational work on which much of this movement's beliefs is based, *Healing the Family Tree* by Dr Kenneth McAll (London: Sheldon, 1986), does – despite its proposition of the doctrine of 'ancestral sin', not found in Catholic teaching – relate a moving story (p. 97) about an old man of seventy-eight 'who had been a deaf mute all his life, [who] suddenly sat up in his bed, his usually unsmiling face alight with happiness, raised both arms and with his last breath shouted "Father".'

9   *Deus Caritas Est*, 38.

10   CCC, 336, citing St Basil.

Postscript: In the Heart of the Father

1   Benedict XVI, General Audience, 23 May 2012.

2   This verse should be read in conjunction with Ephesians 3:14 (quoted at the end of the previous chapter) – Paul kneels before the Father 'from whom every family [literally *fatherhood*], whether spiritual or natural, takes its name' – and 1 John 2:13: 'I am writing to you, fathers, who have come to know the one who has existed since the beginning.' Curiously, I've never heard anyone suggest we should stop calling

educators 'teachers', even though Jesus commands this in the next verse (Mt 23:10).

3   From the hymn 'Alleluia, Sing to Jesus' by William Chatterton Dix (1837–98).

4   John Paul II, Homily at Closing Mass, World Youth Day, Toronto, 28 July 2002.

5   To foster a rediscovery of the Father's loving presence as he watches over the Church of his Son, it would be appropriate to add a feast day in honour of God the Father to the liturgical calendar. Cardinal Raniero Cantalamessa OFM Cap (Preacher to the Papal Household) is one voice among many proposing such a feast in our times.

6   From the Greek verb *sphallein* (to trip up) with privative (negating) 'a-', so *asphalt* is what prevents us from tripping up!

7   The Hebrew consonants of the word *amen* (אמן) are the root letters of the word *emunah*, meaning belief or trust.

8   Talmud: *Shabbat* 119b and *Berachot* 53b.

9   Mary Healy, *Healing: Bringing the Gift of God's Mercy to the World*, Huntingdon, IN: OSV, 2015, p. 194. In this book, Dr Healy (a seminary professor of Scripture and member of the Pontifical Biblical Commission) offers an inspiring study of healing for those wishing to develop their understanding of the subject.

10   CCC, 1505, quoting Matthew 8:17.

11   Nigel Woollen, *The Lamb Will Conquer: Reflections on the Knock Apparition*, Dublin: Veritas, 2017, pp. 25–38.

12   Francis, *Patris Corde*, 7, quoting Matthew 5:45.

13   Francis, *Patris Corde* (conclusion).

Appendix: The Lord's Prayer and the Sacraments

1   With the obvious exception of widowed persons who remarry. The order suggests that the practice of celebrating confirmation before first holy communion (as in the Eastern Churches) has an inherent logic, but an in-depth study of this question would require another book.

2   As stated in chapter 5, the Eucharist is not designated a sacrament of healing by the Church, yet surely its healing powers surpass that of all the others.